basic
VST
INSTRUMENTS

PAUL WHITE

Also by Paul White from Sanctuary Publishing

Audigy – The User Guide
Desktop Digital Studio
Creative Recording I – Effects & Processors
Creative Recording II – Microphones, Acoustics,
    Soundproofing & Monitoring
Home Recording Made Easy (Second Edition)
MIDI For The Technophobe
Live Sound For The Performing Musician
Recording & Production Techniques
Music Technology – A Survivor's Guide

Also in this series

basic DIGITAL RECORDING
basic EFFECTS AND PROCESSORS
basic HOME STUDIO DESIGN
basic LIVE SOUND
basic MASTERING
basic MICROPHONES
basic MIDI
basic MIXERS
basic MIXING TECHNIQUES
basic MULTITRACKING
basic VST EFFECTS

contents

chapter 3

Printed in the United Kingdom by MPG Books Ltd, Bodmin, Cornwall

Published by: Sanctuary Publishing Limited, Sanctuary House, 45-53 Sinclair Road, London
W14 0NS, United Kingdom.
www.sanctuarypublishing.com

ISBN: 1-86074-360-9

chapter 4

introduction

Synthesisers traditionally come as either keyboard instruments or rack-mounted expander modules, but today you can also use instruments in the form of software plug-ins that work within the most popular MIDI/audio sequencers and audio-editing programs, all drawing their power from the host computer. Although software instruments of one kind or another have been available for some years, the turning point for the mass-market user was Steinberg's VST (Virtual Studio Technology) initiative. Part of the VST concept is that additional functionality can be added to a host program by means of these software plug-ins. The current VST standard allows both VST effects and VST instruments to be used.

VST plug-ins are currently very popular because, once Steinberg opened up the VST protocol to third-party companies, it was embraced by many of the major players in the audio software world, and because the VST format relies entirely on the host computer's processor and memory for its operation, no additional hardware is needed to use plug-in effects or instruments. Today, many third-party companies market extremely sophisticated VST instruments, ranging from emulators of vintage organs, pianos and synthesisers to ambitious new designs utilising a variety of synthesis methods. VST instruments also include samplers, which are often easier to use than their hardware counterparts while still offering all of the power and flexibility that a serious user needs, including the ability to read existing sample libraries.

The aim of this book is to explore the ways in which VST instruments can be used within modern MIDI/audio music software and to examine some of the synthesis methods on offer. I'll also be taking a closer look at individual VST instruments that I feel have been particularly successful. However, this isn't a comprehensive guide to the VST instruments currently available, as the list is always growing. As computers continue to become more powerful, it's my feeling that more of the functions of traditional electronic instruments will be integrated into software format, resulting in smaller, more powerful music-recording systems becoming available at lower prices than ever before.

introduction to VST instruments

In the traditional recording studio, synthesisers, MIDI modules, samplers and drum machines come as separate hardware instruments or rack-mounted units, but today you can choose from a number of software-based instruments that can be accessed from within many of the more popular audio programs and MIDI/audio sequencers. Software synthesis is hardly new, but until powerful desktop computers became available to the musician/studio owner at affordable prices, software synthesisers were more academic curiosities than practical tools, and it was often difficult or impossible to integrate such "soft" instruments into other audio programs.

No real progress was made for users of MIDI/audio sequencers users until the German music software manufacturer Steinberg developed their Virtual Studio Technology system, initially to work with their Cubase VST "MIDI-plus-audio" sequencer platform. The result was Cubase VST, which was originally able to run VST effects plug-ins and then, after the introduction of VST II (an update that allowed plug-ins to read MIDI data), VST instruments.

Steinberg quickly opened up their VST protocol to third-party developers so that different software companies could create new effects and instrument plug-ins that could be used within Cubase VST, but then they went one step further and allowed designers of other sequencers and audio programs to make use of the VST protocol as well. This seemingly altruistic move was of huge benefit to computer music makers and software developers alike, as it expanded the potential market enormously. Now, developers only have to develop one version of their plug-ins (well, actually one version for Mac OS and one for PC/Windows) for use in any VST-compatible program. Users in turn benefit from greater choice and lower costs, because of the economy of large-scale production.

Not every audio software company supports the VST protocol directly, although Steinberg (Cubase, Cubasis and Nuendo), Emagic (Logic Audio), Berkley Systems (Bias Peak) and TC Works (Spark and Spark XL) all do. Opcode's Studio Vision software also supports VST, although Mark Of The Unicorn's Digital Performer has its own plug-in format called MAS, and Cakewalk's Sonar software also uses its own plug-in protocol (although either can still use VST plug-ins via suitable adaptor software). The vast majority of serious music programs – including all of those mentioned so far – run on either Macintosh or PC/Windows computers, and sometimes versions of the same audio software are made available for both platforms, as in the case of Cubase VST, Logic Audio and Digital Performer. Different versions of VST plug-ins are required depending on whether the host software runs on a Mac or PC, but most serious plug-ins are supplied with both versions on the same installation disk. However, be aware that there are some Macintosh plug-ins that aren't available for PCs and vice versa.

The original VST format – which could only be used to add VST effects – later evolved into VST II, which provided plug-ins with the ability to read MIDI and tempo information directly from host sequencers. In the case of VST effects, this opened up the possibility of plug-in automation via MIDI, while it also made it possible to build VST instruments such as synthesisers and samplers that could be played via MIDI just like hardware instruments. Those instruments that include sequencing capabilities can automatically lock to the tempo of a sequencer via the VST II protocol.

going native

VST effect and instrument plug-ins are said to be *native* because they rely entirely on the host computer's processor and memory for their operation. Naturally, this means that, the more plug-ins you want to run at the same time, the more of your computer's processing power will be required, and even a fast, modern computer has its limits, in this respect. The amount of power available to new computers seems to double every year or so, but there must always be a limit to the number of VST effects and instruments that you can run inside your sequencer or whatever audio program you're using. However, if you use your plug-ins sensibly, you shouldn't find this too limiting, although it's my feeling that hardware MIDI instruments and VST instruments will continue to co-exist for a number of years yet. Some VST plug-ins require more processing power than others, so if you're using a CPU-hungry VST reverb in your mix, there'll be less power available to use for your VST instruments. Similarly, some VST instruments take a lot more processing power than others, so you'll always have to keep an eye on your CPU usage meter to make sure that you don't push your computer too hard.

advantages of VST instruments

VST instrument plug-ins have several advantages over their hardware equivalents, not least in the fact that they don't need to be run from physical MIDI interface ports. Also, VST instruments appear in the same virtual mixer as audio tracks, so you don't need an external hardware mixer to combine audio and synth-based sounds, unless you're also using hardware instruments. VST instrument plug-ins may also be used in combination with VST effect plug-ins, in which case you don't need to worry about how to route the VST instrument through an external effects processor. (You can still do this, however, if you want to using a multi-output soundcard.)

VST effects and instruments need no wiring, so there's no need for patchbays or cables; they don't take up space in your studio; they don't get dusty or chipped; and they don't wear out or develop component faults. By using them, it also means that you get to avoid crackling cables, ground-loop hum and distortion caused by dirty patchbay connections. In fact, the sound quality of a VST instrument or effect is limited only by the quality of your soundcard. Furthermore, both VST effects and instrument settings can be saved along with song data, so you can get a mix back exactly as you left it without wondering where the volume knob was originally set on your hardware synth or mixer.

With hardware effects boxes, you pay for one and you get one, but with VST plug-ins you still pay for one but you can use as many instances of it simultaneously as your computer's available CPU power can support. This also makes VST plug-ins easier to be used in multitimbral operation than hardware instruments, because in most instances you simply open up a new synth channel each time you want to add another part – you don't have to concern yourself with multi set-ups or similar arcane procedures. For example, you can load up a sampler plug-in on half a dozen different channels, each playing back different sets of samples and with different parameter settings. The only limit to the number of times that a VST plug-in instrument may be used at once is the amount of DSP (Digital Signal Processing) power and RAM available.

disadvantages of VST instruments

The downside of using VST instruments is that, at some point, the computer will throw up its hands and tell you that it can't run any more plug-ins, whereas with traditional hardware you can add as many MIDI instruments to a system as you have MIDI ports available. Some users also complain that they don't like having to use the computer's mouse to adjust the parameters, as they can't adjust more than one at a time. However, to be fair, there are cheap MIDI hardware controllers available for those who want to record dynamic parameter changes in real time. Personally, I prefer the virtual representation of a traditional knobs-and-buttons user interface to the usual cursor controls and mini LCD windows provided on most hardware instruments.

Other negative aspects of using VST instruments include their lack of trade-in value and the fact that they can be used only with software that supports them, unlike hardware synths, which can be used in any MIDI system. On balance, though, VST instruments represent good value for money, and they don't wear out or grow old. They're certainly a welcome addition to the sonic armoury.

types of VST instrument

Virtually any method of hardware synthesis can be implemented in software form, even digital emulations of classic analogue instruments such as the original tape-based sample playback instrument, the Mellotron!

basic VST instruments

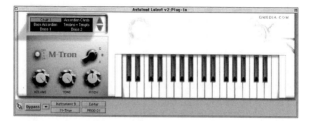

Figure 1.1: G Media's M-Tron plug-in

Figure 1.1 shows G Media's M-Tron plug-in, which comes complete with a selection of soundbanks taken from original Mellotron tapes. Not only have they kept the original eight-second note limit imposed by the original tapes, but they've also added coffee stains on the lid of their virtual instrument!

All modern digital synthesisers are really dedicated music computers, so there's little difference between the results that can be achieved by using dedicated hardware and those that are produced by algorithms running on computers. The use of mathematical modelling has also made it possible to replicate some of the more musically endearing anomalies of vintage instruments, such as filter distortion, tube-amplifier overdrive, the mechanical action noise of certain electric pianos and so on. Many virtual instruments also

18

include some form of effects section, comprising elements such as amp distortion, rotary speaker cabinet emulation, phasers, echo and reverb.

One exciting aspect of VST instrument plug-ins is that software designers can now indulge their imaginations and create new instruments that might never see the light of day as hardware products. Part of the reason why this is possible is that computers can provide any kind of graphical user interface without incurring the costs of tooling and manufacture. Often, the most elaborate instruments are built by software engineers who have a real passion for what they do, and in a hardware-based company they'd have to convince their department head that such a product would sell in sufficient numbers to recoup the manufacturing costs. With software, however, if the engineer is prepared to put in the hours, he can complete the entire project on his own.

software protection

One of the main problems for software companies is piracy, because if nobody pays for the products then the company can't stay in business. No user likes anti-piracy systems, as they usually involve some inconvenience (for the legitimate user, too), but it has been demonstrated that such measures are necessary to

prevent wholesale copying. It might seem like a
victimless crime to give a copy of some music software
to your friends, but if unlawful software copying isn't
checked then there's no incentive for companies to
design new products for us to use, and then we'll all
lose out. In any event, if you really *do* want something
for nothing, there are a number of talented individuals
out there creating their own VST instruments which
they then make available as shareware, usually via CD-
ROMs found on the covers of Internet magazines. One
very worthwhile freebie is the MDA piano, which is
loosely based on the old Yamaha EMT-10 piano module.
Figure 1.2 shows its deceptively simple control panel.

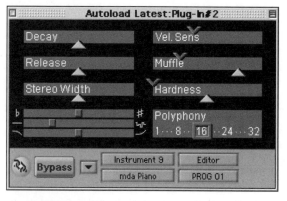

Figure 1.2: MDA piano plug-in

You should also be aware that a lot of pirated – so-called "cracked" – software fails to work properly and may even corrupt legitimately installed software or cause computer instability. There's also a real chance of picking up computer viruses when downloading software (legitimate or otherwise) from the Internet, so if you want to stay safe you should steer clear of pirated software and also use a virus checker if your music computer is also used to access the Internet.

Software protection comes in several forms, the most common for VST plug-ins being the uncopyable master CD-ROM or the challenge-and-response code. Some software is also authorised by means of a master key floppy disk, but such systems are being phased out, as floppy drives are now virtually obsolete.

disk-based protection

Key-disk-install copy protection relies on the use of an uncopyable master floppy disk from which the software is installed. The master disk includes a counter that is decremented when the software is installed and incremented when the software is uninstalled. During the installation procedure, a hidden file is placed on the computer's hard drive, ensuring that the software will work only on that particular computer. When there are no more installations left on the disk, the only way to get it to work again is to uninstall the software, again using the master disk.

If you need to change computers or reformat your hard drive, you'll first have to uninstall all of your copy-protected software. Note that users of Macintosh G4s or other Apple models that use external USB floppy drives may need software patches to enable their drives to authorise their software. Most software of this kind is protected by a system developed by PACE, and the patch you'll need can be downloaded from www.paceap.com.

CD copy protection

The system of using an uncopyable CD-ROM as a master disk is less intrusive than using a master floppy disk, and also the disks are less prone to becoming damaged or corrupted. This is the system used for the installation of virtually all VST instruments. With this procedure, the software is installed from this master CD-ROM in the normal way, but on random occasions (usually when starting up the program) the user is asked to insert the master CD-ROM before he can continue working. More polite software gives you a period of grace during which you can continue working before you're requested to insert the CD-ROM.

challenge and response

Once you've installed software that relies on challenge-and-response security codes, a set of seemingly random words, numbers or characters is generated that is unique to your computer system. These need to be emailed or faxed to the software manufacturer, who will then issue you with another set of codes to type into your computer that will authorise your software to run on your particular computer. You'll usually get a week or two to use the software prior to authorising it, after which the program will time out if you fail to enter the correct response code.

installing plug-ins

VST plug-ins are easy to install, on the whole, as versions for both Macintosh and Windows come complete with largely automated installation routines. There are a few exceptions, however, and in these cases you'll need to follow the manufacturer's instructions particularly carefully. The most important thing to remember is to make sure that your plug-ins are placed in the folder that's used by your audio software named "VstPlugins". If, after installation, your plug-in isn't available from within the Plug-ins menu, check the installation routine and make sure that all of the support files are where they should be.

If the software is copy protected, as most commercial music software is, the first time you start up the software you should see a message on the screen telling you exactly what to do. Some software requires you to enter a serial number, and this number is often found on the software packaging or on the paperwork inside the box. These pieces of paper are easy to lose, so I always take the precaution of writing the serial number on the label side of the installation disk with a felt-tipped marker pen. It might also be wise to create a Notepad file on the computer and keep copies of all of your serial numbers and challenge-and-response codes there, too.

Those using dual-processor Macintosh G4s should note that not all VST plug-ins will work in Dual Processor mode and will frequently cause the computer to lock up or crash. If you experience this problem, either switch off the computer's Dual Processor mode or temporarily remove any incompatible plug-ins from the "VstPlugins" folder before running the audio software that uses them.

computing power

The ability to access high-quality VST instruments on a host computer is very attractive, but I must stress that you'll need to obtain the most powerful computer that you can afford in order to make the most of them.

Don't go by the minimum system requirements quoted for your software, as this really is the bare minimum specification needed to enable the host software to run at all. Furthermore, as your system evolves and you add more plug-ins, you'll eventually need to upgrade your computer. Given that a state-of-the-art PC can cost little more than a typical hardware synth, this isn't such a bad trade-off, considering the extra plug-in power you'll have at your disposal after you upgrade. For instance, always make sure that you have more RAM at your disposal than the minimum specified, and use the CPU usage meter in your audio software to find out what percentage of your computer's power is being used by your plug-ins. Given that RAM is now so inexpensive, it makes sense to install another 256MB over and above what you need to run your basic software.

Also, don't push your computer to the limit, or it will crash at the most inconvenient moment. One useful tip is to zoom out of your sequencer's song window so that the whole song is visible at once. This will avoid the peak in CPU drain that usually occurs whenever the screen is forced to scroll or redraw. Sometimes, this simple trick can make the difference between your computer running smoothly and falling over during audio playback, at which time the CPU is already heavily loaded.

turbo VST instruments?

It would be nice if someone could develop a cheap VST accelerator card to fit into a computer's PCI slot, thus enabling the system to host more VST plug-ins. I've asked several manufacturers in the field why this can't be done, and the gist of their answer is that it wouldn't be practical at anything like a realistic price. The problem is that the CPU in your computer uses *floating-point mathematics*, while most of the high-speed DSP chips that could be used to build a PCI accelerator work on *fixed-point arithmetic*. This means that the VST plug-in software would have to be completely re-written for it to work on a DSP card, in which case it would no longer be a standard DSP plug-in. Nevertheless, at the time of writing, at least two companies are building DSP cards that are designed to run specially written plug-ins that can be accessed from within a VST environment, and one of these is a floating-point system. Therefore, even though they're not really VST plug-ins, they can be used as if they were and accessed from within any VST-compatible program. These cards can provide rather more plug-in processing power than host computers, which is good news if you want to run processor-intensive effects or instruments.

Even if the only VST plug-ins made available for these cards are VST effects (as they may well be, in the early days), it might still be worth using them, as the more VST effects you offload onto the card, the more native CPU power you have at your disposal to use for VST instruments. It's my feeling that, as these "turbo" cards use DSP chips, the manufacturers most likely to write synth plug-ins for them are those who already build DSP-based hardware instruments or those who currently produce plug-ins for high-end DSP-powered systems, such as Digidesign's Pro Tools. The reasoning behind this is that there would be much less work involved in translating DSP hardware algorithms into plug-ins for DSP cards, whereas companies writing native floating-point code for Macs and PCs would have a lot more work to do in order to recompile their algorithms to run on DSPs.

pseudo VST?

Some software companies, such as Emagic, produce their own format of plug-in that works in all respects like a VST plug-in, except that they can only be used within the host application and not within other VST-compatible programs from other manufacturers. Logic Audio, for example, comes complete with several plug-in effects that can be used in the same way as VST effects and may be freely mixed with true VST effects, although they're not actually VST plug-ins at all. Emagic

Figure 1.3: Emagic's EXS-24 sampler plug-in

also produce a range of optional plug-in instruments
that follow the same route, although some of their
plug-in instruments are now available as true VST plug-
ins as well. Figure 1.3 shows the Emagic EXS-24
sampler, which is now also available as a VST plug-in.

practical issues

atency is a problem that's not always understood by those who have recently switched from hardware- to software-based systems, but it's a very important concept to understand, especially if you're using VST instruments. When monitoring what you're recording into a computer-based system (usually via headphones), you may notice a slight delay or echo because of the time delays that are inherent to the system, and this effect is known as latency. Latency is something that occurs when analogue audio is recorded into a computer, when the signal is converted to digital data and then routed via the computer's PCI buss and CPU before being passed on to the soundcard outputs. The magnitude of this delay depends on the operating speed of the computer, the efficiency of the software driver and the amount of RAM buffering that's needed to ensure reliable audio performance, but there will always be some delay. This latency delay is compensated for on playback, but when you're actually recording it can affect your ability to sing or play in time, especially if it's longer than 10ms or so.

ASIO and ASIO II

ASIO stands for Audio Streaming Input/Output and is a driver standard defined by Steinberg to provide low-latency interfacing between audio hardware and software. Other companies are also allowed to use the ASIO format, and so, like VST, it has become a widely adopted standard. ASIO was soon followed by ASIO II, which provides direct *thru monitoring* of the signal being recorded in order to avoid the latency issue (although this doesn't help in the case of virtual instruments). With thru monitoring, the input being recorded is automatically fed directly to the output of the soundcard, so that it can be monitored without going through the computer at all. In this case, when new audio parts are overdubbed, the tracks that are already recorded can be monitored when mixed in with the live sound of a vocal mic or instrument.

It's rather different when you come to play a VST instrument from a keyboard, however, because in this case the instrument sound is actually generated within the CPU itself, so clearly you can't bypass the CPU and still hear the VST instrument you're playing. For a VST instrument to be playable in real time, you ideally need a system that has a latency of less than 7ms, or you'll feel an off-putting lag while you're playing, especially when playing a sound with a fast attack, such as piano. The only real workaround for this problem (if you have a system that can't achieve low latency values) is to record the instrument part using a regular hardware MIDI sound source as a guide and then switch the track back to the VST instrument during playback.

You should note, however, that, although ASIO drivers generally provide the lowest latency figures, drivers specific to a particular pieces of audio software – such as Emagic's EASI driver protocol – may provide you with better results. As a general rule, you should avoid buying a soundcard for use with VST instruments if it doesn't come supplied with a properly functioning ASIO driver or a high-performance driver specific to the VST-compatible audio software that you're using.

In some cases, it's possible to set a lower latency time during recording and then increase this when you come to play back your complete mix in order to avoid running into any audio glitching. As a rule, the more audio tracks and virtual instruments that you have playing back at once, the more you'll need to increase the size of the playback buffer (and hence the latency value) in order to achieve stable operation.

sample rates

The sound-generating engines of some VST instruments – such as Native Instruments' Dynamo and Reaktor – offer a choice of sample rates. As a rule, using a lower sample rate decreases the amount of CPU power demanded by the plug-in, but this may also compromise the instrument's sound quality. The final output sample rate from the instrument you're using will be converted to the value that has been set in the Audio Preferences menu for the current hardware set-up – for instance, if your sequencer is using a sample rate of 44.1kHz and the virtual instrument is outputting at 32kHz, all of your audio output will still be at 44.1kHz. If you're doing serious audio work, you should ideally use a sample rate somewhere between 32kHz and the rate at which your audio hardware is running.

deployment

Obviously, Steinberg's Cubase VST supports VST instruments, as does its "lite" counterpart, Cubasis, and Steinberg's own Neon, VB1 and LM9 VST instrument plug-ins are also included as standard with most variations of the program. Neon is a basic polyphonic synth, while the VB1 is a bass synth plug-in with a visual user interface that looks like the body of a guitar. Instead of adjusting its parameters directly, you can change things like the virtual picking position along the length of the strings. The LM9, meanwhile, is a scaled-down version of Steinberg's LM4 drum module plug-in, played via nine virtual drum pads, that has the ability to create a useful range of contemporary electronic drum sounds. Although these plug-ins aren't really state of the art in terms of sound quality, they are very useful, nonetheless, and they don't demand too much CPU power.

VST instruments are accessed from within Cubase's MIDI instrument tracks, while in Logic Audio special instrument channels are set up in the Audio Mixer page and the desired VST instrument is then loaded into an insert point in the same way as a VST effect. One important point to note is that, in Logic Audio up to at least version 4.7, there is no bank change facility for VST instruments, so some plug-ins can't be used to their full advantage. For example, with Steinberg's LM4, only the first bank of electronic drum sounds are accessible, with the subsequent banks of high-quality sampled sounds remaining out of reach.

Figure 2.1 shows a VST instrument configured within a Cubasis song track, while Figure 2.2 shows how the same plug-in is accessed in Logic Audio.

quality

While the "free" VST instruments provided by
Steinberg and other companies may give you a good
feel for what it's possible to achieve, commercial VST
instruments are often far more sophisticated and
better sounding. You may wonder why some take so
much more processing power when others seem
relatively efficient. The fact is that this isn't always
down to how efficiently the programmers write the
code. On the Mac platform, software for G4s and later

Figure 2.1: VST instrument plug-in accessed in Cubase

models needs to be specially written to take advantage
of the Altivec speed engine incorporated by these
models, and so non-optimised software running on
these machines will be somewhat slower.

A great deal also depends on exactly how the virtual
instrument oscillators are generated within the
program. Those that work from sampled waveforms
are fairly efficient, but they can suffer from aliasing
problems on high notes, giving rise to dissonant or
metallic overtones. On the other hand, those that use
specialist algorithms to generate the oscillators from

Figure 2.2: VST instrument plug-in accessed in Logic Audio

scratch can achieve much of the smoothness of true analogue oscillators, although this is at the cost of demanding more CPU power. Furthermore, virtual instruments with many stages of filtering, modulation or envelope shaping will take more power than simpler instruments, as will those that include their own effects.

presets

Most VST instruments come equipped with a range of preset sounds to get you started, and as with hardware synths, there are some people who use the presets for almost everything. When you first install the software, make sure that any additional files relating to these presets are stored where the program documentation says they should be stored (which is usually in the "VstPlugins" folder), or you may find yourself unable to access them.

When you edit a preset, you'll often find a Compare option that lets you switch back and forth between the original and edited versions of the patch. For those who are less confident at synth programming, a useful way of building up a library of customised patches is to make small adjustments to presets and then save the edited version under a new name.

compatibility issues

Just occasionally, you may come across a combination
of VST instruments or VST effects that causes the
computer to crash. One well-known cause is the use of
plug-ins that aren't optimised for dual processors in a
Macintosh G4 dual processor computer with Dual
Processor mode switched on. Often, the only solution
to this is to remove the offending plug-in from the
"VstPlugins" folder or to set the machine to Single
Processor mode. In other instances, it may be just that
two VST plug-ins refuse to co-exist. This doesn't
happen often, but I've had it happen to me on a couple
of occasions, once when a particular VST effect caused
the computer to crash if it was ever placed in an insert
point directly following a VST instrument. All that you
can do is notify the suppliers of the conflicting products
and hope that a future upgrade will resolve the
problem. In the meantime, you'll simply have to resign
yourself to not using the offending plug-ins together.

memory

All plug-ins require some RAM, although some need
more than others. RAM is currently very cheap, so again
you should install a bare minimum of 256MB and ideally
256MB more than you think you're actually going to
need. If you're a Mac user with pre-OS X system

software, you should read the manual that comes with their host sequencer program to find out how much memory needs to be allocated to it and then add to this number the amount needed for additional plug-ins. You might expect that setting aside a huge amount of memory for the program would be playing safe, but paradoxically some programs – such as Emagic's Logic Audio – seem just as unhappy if they're given too much memory as they are when given too little.

Other VST instruments, such as samplers, may use memory not allocated to the host program, so again you should check the manual. I know that, if you install a new VST instrument and it appears to work, it's tempting to leave the settings as they are, but if you do this you may run into difficulties when you try to run several VST instruments in the same song. In most instances, you can read through the manual once and then put it on away the shelf, but with some of the more complicated VST instruments it's a good idea to keep the manuals nearby, as some aspects of sound editing may not be obvious, especially if you've had little experience of synth editing before.

synthesis methods

The majority of VST instruments are synthesisers, and most of these work on principles that have already been proven in the hardware arena. In theory, any type of hardware synthesiser can be emulated in software, provided that there's enough processing power available to do the job, but the current fascination with vintage analogue instruments means that this was one of the first areas to be exploited by designers of software instruments. The function of this chapter is to provide an overview of the most important synthesis methods so that, when you enter the wonderful world of VST instruments, you'll feel confident enough to create or edit a few patches of your own rather than have to rely on the presets provided by the manufacturer.

The first mainstream electronic keyboard instrument was the electronic organ, and on this device, by combining the outputs from oscillators tuned to different harmonics, it was possible to create a number of different waveform shapes that roughly corresponded to those produced by "real" acoustic instruments. However, unlike most acoustic instruments, the electronic organ plays all notes at a fixed level, with nothing more elaborate than a master-level control pedal to add expression. Furthermore, an organ note starts abruptly whenever a key is pressed and stops equally abruptly when that key is released. As with most instruments that have limitations, this gave rise to new playing styles, and the electronic organ became a new instrument in its own right. However, it never had a future in providing realistic imitations of acoustic instruments.

An excellent example of an organ plug-in is the Native Instruments B4, which uses modelling techniques to emulate the behaviour of the tone wheels, the keyboard-switching network and the rotary speakers of the original. On this plug-in, even the overload characteristics of the valve amplifier and the distance of the microphone from the speaker are modelled with great accuracy. Figure 3.1 shows the control panel of the B4 plug-in. Note that this particular plug-in can work on three MIDI channels at once to provide access to the upper and lower manuals and to the bass pedals.

Acoustic instruments tend to evolve by trial and error, and in many cases the mechanism of sound production

Figure 3.1: B4 Tonewheel Organ

is quite complex, with many factors influencing the final result. For example, a piano's sound starts quite abruptly as the hammers hit the strings and then dies away progressively as the vibrating strings lose energy. A bowed violin or cello, on the other hand, can have an abrupt attack or a slow attack, depending on the way it's played, and when the bow is removed, the string vibrations die away over a short period of time. Where a note is produced by applying an impulse to a resonant system, such as the plucking of a string, the level of the note will decay after being plucked and the harmonic structure may also change as the note decays. In most instances, high frequencies die away faster than low frequencies, so natural sounds have a tendency to sound progressively duller as they decay. Figure 3.2 shows the envelope of a typical percussive sound, while Figure 3.3 shows the envelope of a bowed sound.

sound

In electronic music production with synthesisers or VST instruments, no sound actually exists until a signal is fed into a loudspeaker or a pair of headphones. This electronic signal produced by the instrument carries all of the harmonic and pitch information that defines the sound.

We all know that sound is produced by vibrations in the air that cause the eardrum to move slightly and that these movements are translated by the human brain into the sensation that we know as sound. Sound travels outwards from its point of origin, and the intensity of the sound reduces as the wavefront expands to cover an ever larger area. Sound can be thought of as a three-dimensional equivalent of ripples on a pond. The spacing between consecutive ripples determines the pitch of the sound, while the rate at

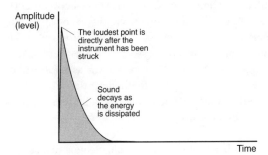

Figure 3.2: Typical percussion sound envelope

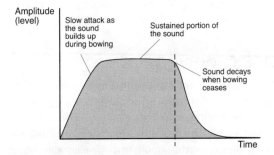

Figure 3.3: Typical bowed string sound envelope

which these ripples occur is the sound's frequency. The human hearing range lies somewhere between 20Hz and 20kHz, depending on the condition and age of the ears doing the listening, although most musically significant information lies between 50Hz and 12kHz. Multiples of 1,000 cycles are known as *kiloHertz* or *kHz*. The higher the frequency, the higher the perceived musical pitch, and a doubling in pitch is known as an *octave*.

Pitch is obviously a very important element of music, as it allows us to create melodies, harmonies and chords, but there's a lot more to sound than pitch. If that weren't the case, any two instruments playing the same note would sound identical, which they clearly don't. So what defines the character of a musical sound, other than pitch?

basic waves

The simplest sound is a pure tone comprising a single frequency. The changes in air pressure caused by the production of a pure tone can be plotted on a piece of paper to produce a graph like that shown in Figure 3.4, which illustrates the graph of a familiar sine wave. (Note that, in musical terms, a sine wave sounds exactly the same as a cosine wave. Only the starting

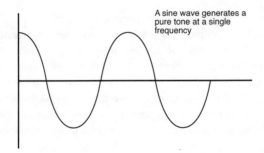

A sine wave generates a pure tone at a single frequency

Figure 3.4: Pure-tone sine wave

point of the waveform on the graph is different.) The electrical output of a microphone recording this sound would also be a sine wave, so an electrical signal representing a sound simply replaces a modulation of air pressure with a modulation of voltage. The electrical signal is analogous to the sound, hence the term *analogue*.

A continuous sine wave sounds like a pure whistle, where every cycle of the waveform is identical. It doesn't sound that great as a musical source, of course, but it is the most basic of all waveforms and it's important to understand it. A sine wave consists only of a fundamental pitch and a level, but the sounds of acoustic instruments are much more complex.

Rather than producing pure sine waves (although flutes can come close), acoustic instruments generate a whole range of related frequencies known as *harmonics* and *overtones*. Harmonics are frequencies that are exact multiples of the basic or fundamental pitch, while non-harmonic overtones may be thought of as harmonics that aren't exact multiples of the fundamental pitch. Instruments that use pairs of strings tuned in unison – such as pianos and twelve-string guitars or those that use metal resonators, such as bells – produce strong overtones. Even the sounds of instruments that are perceived to produce only a single pitch often contain some overtones. While it's relatively simple to synthesise harmonics, overtones are less easy to control.

Most musical sounds have a well-defined fundamental frequency, which is taken to be the musical pitch of the note. This is accompanied by a series of harmonics that are higher in frequency (ie pitch) but generally lower in level than the fundamental. If the harmonics are even multiples of the fundamental, they're known as *even harmonics*, whereas, if they're odd multiples, they're known as *odd harmonics*. Figure 3.5 shows how the harmonic series is constructed. It is possible for an instrument to generate harmonics that go far beyond the limit of human hearing.

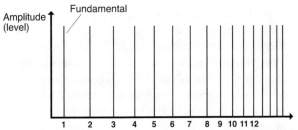

Harmonic series for the note A 110Hz as
far as the tenth harmonic. Note that all
of the harmonics are shown as being of
equal amplitude. This would not be the
case for naturally generated sounds

Harmonic	Frequency
Fundamental (A)	110Hz
Second	220Hz
Third	330Hz
Fourth	440Hz
Fifth	550Hz
Sixth	660Hz
Seventh	770Hz
Eighth	880Hz
Ninth	990Hz
Tenth	1,100Hz

Each harmonic in the series is a whole-
number multiple of the fundamental

Figure 3.5: The harmonic series (odd and even)

timbre or quality

The character of a sound is determined partly by its harmonic structure, but the balance of harmonics and overtones will tend to change as the sound evolves. The pitch of the overtones may also change slightly. This happens if a string is plucked hard, causing it to start slightly sharp before falling back to its tuned pitch as it decays. The lesson to be learned here is that the sounds of real instruments are dynamic events, forever changing as the notes evolve or decay. The electronic organ, on the other hand, tends to produce notes with fixed harmonic structures, although some models have a facility that allows the user to introduce additional harmonics for a brief period when the note is first struck, which is known as the *organ percussion effect*.

the complexity of reality

The way in which the levels of the different harmonics and overtones decrease in level over time determines the decay portion of the sound's envelope, and each harmonic has its own decay envelope, as no two harmonics will decay at exactly the same rate. Most natural sounds, including those produced by acoustic instruments, have faster decay times at high frequencies simply because high-frequency energy is dissipated more rapidly than low-frequency energy.

Knowing this can be useful when it comes to synthesising natural sounds, although to do the job thoroughly would mean synthesising each harmonic, adjusting its level and then providing each with an individual decay envelope. Furthermore, to get real accuracy, you'd need to be able to control the sound so that it changed in accordance with playing technique, thus matching the behaviour of the acoustic instrument being emulated.

Layering up a sound from scratch in this way is known as *additive synthesis*, and, although technically possible, this is an extremely complex process and therefore expensive to realise and difficult to control. Sophisticated re-synthesis techniques can be used to synthesise a sound from its basic harmonic components, but at the time of writing, this isn't a commonplace method of attempting to emulate real instruments in an electronic environment.

While true additive synthesis requires each harmonic to be created and controlled separately, there are far more approximate techniques that can be used to produce caricatures of real instruments, which is exactly where *analogue synthesis* started out. As it turns out, analogue synthesis can emulate only a limited number of instrument types with any degree of realism. For example, analogue string and brass sounds are quite acceptable, whereas analogue piano and guitar emulations tend to be disappointing. Nevertheless, shortly after its introduction into the commercial music world, the analogue synthesiser was accepted as a new instrument capable of creating its own unique sounds, so it didn't really matter that it couldn't copy the majority of acoustic instruments very convincingly. Analogue synthesis is still very popular today, even though many hardware instruments and all VST plug-ins use digital processing to do what the original instruments did with oscillators, filters, voltage-controlled amplifiers and control voltages.

analogue synthesis

The true analogue synthesiser relies entirely on analogue circuitry, where oscillators, filters and envelope shapers are controlled by electrical waveforms and voltages. It isn't necessary to know how any of this works in detail, but it is helpful to be able to visualise the flow of a signal through the various stages of the instrument, since digital equivalents follow the same paradigm.

Analogue circuitry doesn't posses the inherent stability of modern digital designs, but the subtle detuning effects that were produced were often credited as contributing to the warmth or musicality of the analogue sound. Now, by using digital algorithms, the designer can choose whether to have perfectly stable oscillators or whether to introduce a small degree of random drift in order to emulate more closely the true analogue sound.

The original analogue synths were also monophonic – ie, they could only play one note at a time, where a note typically comprised the outputs from one or two oscillators generating simple, basic waveshapes such as sine, square, triangle, sawtooth or pulse. These instruments had no velocity sensitivity, and whenever a new note was played, the previous note was cut short. Digital instruments, both real and virtual, can easily recreate these limitations, but it's more usual to find polyphony and velocity sensitivity included.

subtractive synthesis

Most of the commonly used methods of synthesis rely on what is known as *subtractive synthesis*, where some sound or waveform is used as a starting point and then unwanted elements are removed by filtering and/or by controlling levels via envelope shapers. Analogue synthesis is a clearly recognisable type of subtractive synthesis, as the process starts out with a harmonically rich basic waveform and filters are then used to change the levels of the various harmonics while voltage-controlled amplifiers are used to control the envelope of the sound. In this respect, subtractive synthesis can be thought of as being like carving something from a piece of wood – you always start out with more than you need and then cut away what isn't wanted.

While the skilled wood carver can add as much fine detail as his patience will allow, analogue synthesisers can only shape the sound in a relatively limited way, as the filters used are relatively simple and the envelope generators can only approximate the envelopes of real instruments. However, the limitations of the analogue synthesiser also contribute to its charm. Virtual analogue synthesisers work in much the same way as their analogue counterparts as regards signal flow, but of course the oscillators, filters and gain-control elements are all implemented digitally. While analogue oscillators tend to drift in pitch slightly with temperature and time, digital oscillators can be made as stable as the highly accurate sample-rate clock that clocks the system, and so near-absolute stability can be achieved. Even so, some designers deliberately introduce small, pseudo-random pitch changes to emulate the way in which analogue instruments behave.

Modern sample-based electronic instruments also follow a subtractive topography, with the main difference being that, instead of using simple waveforms as the source sounds, they use samples of existing acoustic and electronic instrument sounds, plus some more abstract sounds from other sources that are then modified by filters and envelope shapers in much the same was as the signal would be treated in an analogue synthesiser. Steinberg's Model E VST plug-in is closely modelled on the classic MiniMoog synthesiser, which was one of the first commercially available analogue synths and certainly one of the best loved. Figure 3.6 shows the control screen for the Model E.

Figure 3.6: Steinberg's Model E synth plug-in

subtractive elements

All subtractive synthesisers comprise a number of fairly standard processing blocks linked together to produce the desired result, and the first block is invariably the oscillator. Early analogue synthesisers used physically separate modules for the different building blocks, along with summing amplifiers, which meant that the user could experiment with different configurations by using patch cords to link them together. (Incidentally, this is where the term *patch* originated.)

At the heart of any synthesiser is a tone oscillator that produces the basic sound, and even if the source sound is a sample rather than a basic waveform, this device is still referred to as an oscillator. An analogue synthesiser uses true oscillators that generate simple repeating waveforms based on sine, square, pulse, triangle and sawtooth waves. A sine wave generates only a fundamental pitch and so can't be further modified by filtering, as the only result would be a change in level. Meanwhile, square waves comprise only odd harmonics, while sawtooth waves comprise both odd and even harmonics. The harmonic series of a pulse waveform changes in response to the width of the pulse, and as a rule this waveform is useful for creating buzzy or reedy sounds, while the sawtooth wave tends to be used as the basis of the production of string and brass sounds.

Although modular analogue synthesisers can be patched any way the user wishes to try, the traditional topography for a simple analogue synthesiser is an oscillator followed by one filter and either one or two envelope shapers, as shown in Figure 3.7, where the oscillator – which can be switched to produce a number of basic waveshapes – generates the source waveform and determines the balance of odd and even harmonics that the sound will contain. This source waveform then passes through a filter which attenuates some of the harmonics, after which the signal is processed by an envelope shaper, which determines (in its simplest configuration) how quickly the sound builds up after a key is pressed and how fast it decays once the key is released. The other envelope shaper controls how fast the filter opens and closes when a note is played.

This, however, is a very basic model. A more realistic configuration is to have two independently tunable tone oscillators and a third low-frequency oscillator to act as a modulation source to produce tremolo, vibrato and so on, while there will probably also be a noise source available in the oscillator section to synthesise percussion sounds or wind and sea noises.

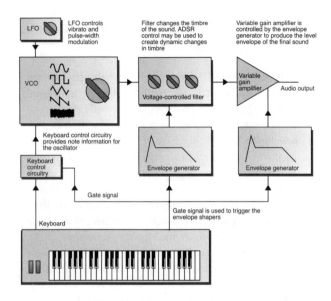

Figure 3.7: Basic analogue synthesiser comprising one oscillator followed by one filter and two envelope shapers

the oscillator

As we've learned, the analogue synthesiser offers a choice of simple geometric waveforms, often with the option of including additional random noise. The waveform of noise looks completely random and contains all audio frequencies at all times. If you were to listen to it without filtering, it sound like loud hiss or a powerful rushing noise. By filtering a signal containing noise, it's possible to simulate the sound of breath noise to add to flute simulations, as well as the sound of wind, surf, snare drums and so on.

There are four main oscillator waveforms used in analogue synthesis:

- Sine waves
- Square or pulse waves
- Triangle waves
- Sawtooth waves

sine waves

The sine wave is a pure tone comprising a fundamental frequency with no harmonics. It's a useful modulation source for adding natural-sounding vibrato or tremolo, but it can also be used as a sound source for synthesising flute sounds or whistling noises. Low-frequency sine waves can also be useful to add depth to sounds produced by other oscillators, which is particularly useful for bass sounds in dance music, and in synthesisers that include distortion effects the sine wave can be made to sound more interesting, as the distortion process introduces harmonics.

square waves

A square wave and a triangle wave both contain a fundamental plus a series of odd harmonics, although the triangle wave has a much lower harmonic content than the square wave. Both produce a hollow, reedy tone, but the square wave sounds much brighter than the triangle wave. Both of these waveforms may be used to synthesise reed instruments such as clarinets, although they're also useful in producing purely synthetic lead and bass sounds.

If the mark/space ratio (ie the ratio of the time that the waveform is at its maximum voltage against the time it's at its minimum voltage) of a square wave is changed from 50/50 so that the waveform becomes a repeating pulse, the balance of odd harmonics is changed. Because many acoustic instruments generate an asymmetrical waveform, the pulse waveform is actually very important. The sound becomes thinner and more buzzy as the pulse is made narrower, which makes it useful for creating reed tones such as oboe sounds. All but the most basic analogue synths and virtual analogue synths allow the pulse width to be controlled from the output of a low-frequency oscillator running at just a few cycles per second. This important effect is known as *pulse-width modulation*, and it sounds very much like two oscillators that aren't quite in tune with each other.

Indeed, if you were to set up two square-wave oscillators running at exactly the same frequency and then detuned one slightly while inspecting the combined waveform with an oscilloscope, you'd see a waveform that would show the pulse width changing as the oscillator became detuned. Pulse-width modulation can produce the same subjective effects with a single tone oscillator, and so it provides an economic way of creating chorus or detuning a signal. It's therefore often used to fatten pad sounds or to create ensemble effects.

sawtooth waves

The sawtooth wave comprises the fundamental plus both odd and even harmonics and is used to create string, brass and many synth pad sounds. If a synthesiser has two or more tone oscillators, these may be set to different waveforms and added in different proportions in order to create a source with a harmonic structure that's different to any of the basic waveforms used individually. Figure 3.8 shows the principal types of waveform available from an analogue oscillator.

Don't worry about the implications of the various waveforms and their harmonic content. Your ear will soon tell you what works best for a particular

basic VST instruments

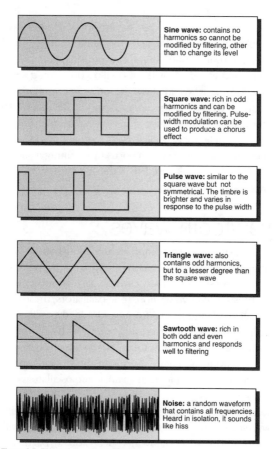

Figure 3.8: The main synth waveforms

60

application. You should also note that most oscillators have switchable ranges, enabling them to be tuned up or down in steps of one octave. This is in addition to a fine-tuning control, which allows you to produce detuning effects. Interesting effects can be created by choosing different waveforms for the two oscillators and then trying one of the oscillators in a different register. Using an interval of an octave often produces organ-like tones.

It's also possible to tune one oscillator higher or lower than the other by, for example, a perfect fifth, and this can produce very fat sounds, especially when combined with suitable filtering. However, you have to be careful with parallel tunings, as they only work in specific musical contexts.

keyboard control

In a hardware analogue synthesiser, the action of pressing a key sends a control voltage to the oscillator to tell it what pitch to produce, and it also produces a gate signal to trigger envelope generators. In a MIDI-controlled digital synthesiser, the MIDI Note number determines the basic oscillator pitch (which can still be shifted by octaves or detuned on the synth itself). The Note On part of this message also triggers the envelope generators. When a Note Off message is received (ie when the key is released), the envelope generator(s) enter the release phase.

The way in which an oscillator in a synth plug-in reacts when a new note is played will depend on whether the synthesiser is monophonic or polyphonic. On a monophonic synth, when another signal is sent, any note that's still sounding (perhaps due to a long release time setting) will be terminated abruptly and the new note will play. In the case of a polyphonic instrument, the original note will continue to sound. However, if you play a rapid passage that leaves more notes sounding than the synth has enough polyphony to accommodate, the oldest notes will be cut off to allow the new ones to play. For example, if you have a synth with six-note polyphony and then you play a seventh note on top of this, the first note you played will be turned off.

One of the best respected polyphonic analogue synthesisers was the Prophet 5, and Native Instruments have paid tribute to this instrument with their Pro-52 plug-in. The control panel on this plug-in is closely based on that of the Prophet 5 hardware synth, and the resulting sound is also surprisingly authentic. Figure 3.9 shows the control window of the Pro-52 plug-in.

Figure 3.9: Native Instruments' Pro-52 plug-in

portamento

Some acoustic instruments, such as the violin, have the
ability to slide from one note to another, while others,
such as the piano, are restricted to a fixed series of
notes. This sliding effect can be emulated in
synthesisers – albeit pretty crudely – by something
called *portamento*.

Portamento is a parameter that sets the rate at which a
tone oscillator can change from one pitch to the next.
When a high value of portamento is used, the oscillator
pitch will glide slowly from the old note to the new note

when a new key is pressed. The portamento time is generally adjustable from almost instantaneous to a gradual slur, and you may find that a fairly rapid portamento is useful for enhancing brass sounds, particularly sounds like trombones.

oscillator phase sync

When I first started to play around with analogue synthesisers, I discovered that some instruments included a function known as *oscillator phase sync*, and I was immediately hooked. Oscillator phase sync is responsible for some of the meanest and nastiest lead synth sounds around! I'm happy to say that many virtual analogue synths and plug-ins have retained this feature, including the Pro-52.

With oscillator phase sync, one oscillator is designated as the master and the other as the slave, and the master oscillator plays the pitch of the melody while the second contributes to the timbre of the sound. The slave oscillator may be tuned to the same frequency as the master oscillator, or to any interval, but the key point is that the slave oscillator's waveform will always be cut short and forced to "restart" whenever a cycle of the master oscillator's waveform is complete. In practice, this means that the slave oscillator is always forced to follow the pitch of the master oscillator, regardless of how it's tuned. The only thing that changes if you attempt to retune it is its waveform and, hence, its harmonic structure.

If the slave oscillator's tuning is increased manually (by using the master keyboard's pitch-bend wheel, for example) while the master remains constant (in which case pitch-bend modulation needs to be switched off on the master oscillator), you can hear the slave oscillator jumping from one harmonic to the next, which produces a dramatic change in timbre. As the pitch-bend wheel is turned, the output signal changes dramatically, producing an effect that sometimes sounds a little like flanging and sometimes like a heavily overdriven electric guitar. You'll hear this effect on a lot on dance records and on albums where the synthesiser takes over the role of lead guitar.

LFOs

LFOs (Low Frequency Oscillators) are very important, as they add a sense of movement to what can otherwise be a very static tone-oscillator sound. The simplest LFO is a sine- or triangle-wave oscillator running at just a few cycles per second, and if you've used the modulation wheel on a synth or keyboard to introduce vibrato then you've already heard one example of what an LFO can do. In this case, the LFO is arranged to modulate the pitch of the tone oscillator, but it could also be routed to the filter cut-off frequency to create a regular wah-wah effect, or it could be used to modulate the synth's output level to produce tremolo. Changing the amount of a signal's LFO modulation will affect the depth of the effect, enabling the user to introduce natural-sounding vibrato to things like flute, violin and cello parts. Of course, it also means that you can add vibrato to purely abstract sounds.

digital synthesis

Although analogue synthesisers eventually evolved to become polyphonic and, later, MIDI controlled, the basic waveforms remained the same until digital synthesisers came along. Digital synthesisers first became commercially viable in the early 1980s and were able to offer far more flexibility than analogue instruments could, and so, within a short space of time, FM synthesis (the Yamaha DX7), wavetable synthesis (the PPG), sampling (the Fairlight and Synclavier) and sample-based synths (the Roland D50 and Korg M1) became available. Digital instruments designed to model the attributes of older analogue models were developed later, during the mid 1990s.

The "oscillator" of a sample-based synth may simply be a one-shot sample, such as a drum beat or a piano note, or it may be a looped sample capable of indefinite sustain, such as a string, choir or synth pad sound. Looped sounds will play for as long as a key is held down because, in most cases, the sound continues as long as the key is held down, whereas a one-shot sound will end when the sample has finished playing. Percussive sounds are normally designed to play through completely, even if the key is released before the sound is complete, as this produces the most natural-sounding result.

In a wavetable-based synthesiser, the oscillator is based on a table of waveforms that may be either related or completely different. Not all wavetable synthesisers work in exactly the same way, but in most an electronic pointer moves through the wavetable, and when it points to a wave, this wave repeats continuously until the pointer moves elsewhere. If the wavetable comprises waves taken at different points in a choral recording, for example, causing the pointer to run up and down the wavetable fairly slowly (via modulation from an LFO or envelope) will produce a reasonably natural vocal effect with an ever-changing timbre. If, on the other hand, the waves in the table aren't related to each other, the sound will change dramatically as the pointer moves along the table. Often, there's some kind of mechanism available for crossfading the transitions so that they don't sound too abrupt.

Subjectively, a wavetable synthesiser working on this principle still sounds "synthetic" but has more of an organic quality than analogue synthesisers, in which the waves generated by the oscillators remain unchanged. Filters and envelope shapers are still used to shape the sound, and so wavetable synthesis is still a method of subtractive synthesis. The classic wavetable synthesiser is the PPG Wave, which also makes an appearance as a Steinberg plug-in complete with the original wavetables. A couple of minor features have been omitted, but on the whole this plug-in both looks and sounds remarkably faithful to the original. The PPG Wave 2 plug-in is shown in Figure 3.10.

Figure 3.10: PPG Wave 2 plug-in

sample-based synthesis

The majority of modern hardware synthesisers that aren't designed specifically to emulate analogue instruments are sample based, inasmuch as the oscillator section is effectively a sample-playback engine. As described earlier, these samples may be looped or one-shot percussive sounds. However, whereas a sampler has access to a large amount of RAM, hardware instruments use sounds that are stored in ROM. This usually means that all the sounds for an instrument have been compressed into 8MB, 16MB or 32MB. When you consider that a well-sampled piano can take up more than 32MB on its own, you can see how restricting this is. Fortunately, sample-based VST instruments can use the RAM fitted to the host computer to load sound waveforms stored on its hard drive, and so memory restrictions are much less of a problem. All General MIDI instruments use sample-based synthesis.

FM synthesis

FM (Frequency Modulation) is a method of synthesis that was explored in academic circles in as early as the 1960s, but it wasn't until Yamaha brought out their DX7 synthesiser, in the early 1980s, that it was brought into the commercial domain. The nature of FM synthesis relies on the fact that, when one audio frequency is modulated by another, the resulting waveform contains both sum and difference frequencies, as well as the two original frequencies. By setting up small networks of oscillators that modulate each other in different ways (Yamaha called these networks *algorithms*), a number of extremely complex sounds can be created. However, the process of sound creation via FM synthesis isn't nearly as intuitive as it is with analogue synthesis. The timbre of the sound may be changed by dynamically changing the depth of FM modulation, again under the control of things like LFOs or envelopes, and the resulting waveform may be processed further by using envelope generators. The DX7 didn't include filters, although there's no reason why an FM instrument shouldn't include them.

FM instruments excel at creating plucked or struck metallic sounds, and it was undoubtedly the superlative electric piano sound that caused the DX7 to sell in such huge quantities. However, while the strengths of FM synths are their piano, bell and hard brass sounds, they are less successful in producing soft pad and strings sounds, although an instrument that combines FM synthesis with traditional filtering is likely to be more effective in this respect.

physical modelling

In a physical-modelling instrument, instead of using an oscillator or a sample as the basic sound source, a mathematical model is used to generate the sound. On an analogue synthesiser, this would be a model of the way in which the oscillators behave, including any imperfections, so that, when you press a key, the waveform is generated in real time rather than read out of a sampled waveform table. The same thing applies to the filters, which model the physical instrument as closely as possible, right down to the types of distortion introduced when the filter is close to being overloaded.

When acoustic instruments are physically modelled, the mechanism of sound production in the original instruments is "gain constructed" as a mathematical model. For example, replicating the sound of a wind instrument might involve simulating the vibration of the reed and the resonance of the tubular body of the instrument. Smaller details can also be modelled, such as the shape of the flare at the end of the instrument or the way in which the mouthpiece connects to the body, and the more rigorous the model, the closer the sound is to that of the real instrument. The advantage of physical modelling is that such an instrument can be made to play very responsively, so that, when you play a flute patch with a high velocity, the sound may

71

change its harmonic structure, just as a real instrument would if overblown. This overcomes the principal limitation of sample-based instruments, which is that the player can only introduce a limited amount of expression into his playing by using pedals, modulation wheels and so on.

Different mathematical models are required for different types of instrument, and it's possible to model many acoustic instruments convincingly, including drums, which require the modelling of a tensioned membrane and a resonant shell. Figure 3.11 shows a block diagram of a physically modelled instrument. A number of VST instruments use modelling to produce a sound that's as close as possible to the real thing, including Native Instruments' B4 plug-in, which models the tone wheels and rotary speakers of the Hammond organ and Leslie speaker.

In theory, modelling can be used to create entirely new types of instrument by combining aspects of existing instruments with those that have never been realised in real life. Although the sound might be unlike anything we've heard before, it should still have the dynamic response of a real instrument. For example, you could use a bowed string as the "oscillator" and then feed this into the model of a didgeridoo.

Instead of an oscillator, the physical-modelling synthesiser may use a driver signal, which is applied to a resonant filter that emulates the body of the instrument. The interaction of these is what creates the characteristic instrument sound

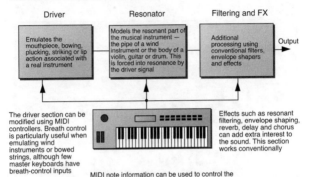

Figure 3.11: Block diagram of a physical-modelling instrument

multi-synthesis

There are VST instrument plug-ins currently available that use each of the above synthesis methods, sometimes in combination with each other, although there are few sample-based synthesiser plug-ins around that rival their hardware counterparts in this respect. One reason for this may be that VST samplers and sample players are now so easy to use and so

Figure 3.12: Native Instruments' Dynamo synth plug-in

powerful that they offer virtually all of the sound-
creation capabilities found on a sample-based
synthesiser but without the same limitations, the main
one being that the user is restricted to using the
samples provided by the designer.

Native Instruments provide two similar packages, one called Dynamo and one called Reaktor, that offer a number of modules that combine synthesis methods. Reaktor can be used to build new synths from scratch, while Dynamo is based on the set of library instruments that's provided with Reaktor. Figure 3.12 shows one of Dynamo's modules, and this one is designed to emulate an analogue synthesiser, while Figure 3.13 shows another Native Instruments plug-in called Absynth, another multi-synthesis device, which is capable of producing an extraordinary range of sounds, from hard leads and basses to strange, evolving pads. Absynth's multi-stage envelope generators are an integral part of its unique approach to sound creation.

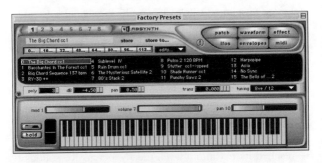

Figure 3.13: Native Instruments' Absynth plug-in

filters and envelopes

Regardless of the type of oscillator that's used in a synth, the resulting signal is usually passed through a filter and invariably through an envelope shaper. On modern digital instruments, the filters and envelope shapers are all implemented by using microcomputer technology, while in a VST instrument they're calculated by the host computer's CPU. Nevertheless, the overall operational concept is similar, regardless of the method of sound generation.

The timbre of a natural sound is dictated by its harmonic content and its level envelope (ie the rate at which the sound builds up and dies away). The envelopes of acoustic instruments can be very complex, but most can be approximated using a four-stage ADSR (Attack, Decay, Sustain and Release) envelope generator. In an analogue synthesiser, this would control the gain of a VCA (Voltage-Controlled Amplifier), but in a digital instrument it's used in a multiplier configuration to change the levels of individual samples.

A standard ADSR envelope is shown in Figure 3.14, where the Attack phase would normally be initiated by the pressing of a key and would last until the sound reached its maximum level. Clearly, percussive sounds therefore produce a very fast attack. Once the attack is

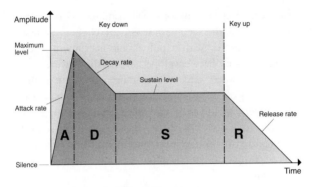

Figure 3.14: Diagram of a typical ADSR envelope

at its maximum level, the Decay phase is initiated, whereupon the level of the sound starts to decay at a rate set by the Decay parameter, until it reaches the Sustain level. (Note that, while Attack and Decay are parameters measured in time, Sustain relates to level.) The envelope remains at the level set by the Sustain parameter for as long as the key is held down, but when the key is released the sound resumes its decay, now at a new rate set by the Release parameter. In the case of a monophonic synthesiser, whenever a new key is depressed before the envelope generator has run its course, a new envelope starts afresh, along with the new note, unless the instrument has a Legato mode, in which case the original envelope will continue to operate, provided that the second note is played before the first one is released. With a polyphonic instrument, each "voice" has its own envelope, and so the playing of a new note won't affect the earlier notes, unless the polyphony of the instrument is exceeded, in which case the older notes will be cut off, a process sometimes known as *note stealing*. Basic ADSR envelope generators are used in most current synthesisers, as are more complex variations, often with more than the four standard stages.

One reason why more complex envelopes are often needed is that many acoustic instruments can't be accurately synthesised by way of a simple ADSR envelope. This is particularly true of ensemble sounds, where the instruments may start playing at slightly different times. A brass ensemble synth patch may be programmed with two or more sharp peaks at the start of the envelope to simulate this effect, as shown in Figure 3.15.

envelope-to-oscillator modulation

Another reason why complex envelopes are sometimes needed is that envelope generators can be used to modulate parameters other than loudness. It's common

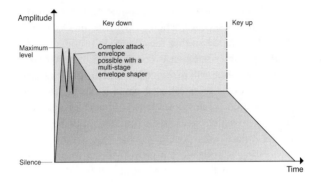

Figure 3.15: Multi-stage envelope showing multiple attack spikes

for envelopes to be used to modulate filter cut-off frequencies, but they may also be used to control the pitches of oscillators, and if many envelope stages are available it's possible to create arpeggiator effects or short melodic sequences. Furthermore, the envelope modulation of pitch can be used to make some instrument emulations sound more natural, such as those wind instruments that start off sharp when blown hard and then fall back to the correct pitch. This effect is easily achieved by using an envelope with a fairly fast attack and decay, although the modulation depth must be adjusted with care so that the change in pitch is fairly subtle, or you'll end up with a sci-fi effect.

Envelopes are also useful for adjusting the pitch of the second oscillator when a synth is in Oscillator Phase Sync mode so that the change in timbre caused by the phase sync effect is consistent for every note. A long envelope will produce a long harmonic sweep effect, whereas a very short envelope can be used to give a sound a harmonically rich attack. In general, the way in which synthesiser functions may be used to modulate each other is the key to creating interesting sounds, so I urge you to set aside some time in which to experiment with your VST instruments rather than relying too much on the factory-supplied presets.

automatic delay vibrato

LFO modulation is often used to control oscillator vibrato (pitch modulation) via the modulation wheel so that it can be brought in progressively to simulate the ways in which many acoustic instruments are played. However, some instruments include a facility that automatic delays vibrato. With this function, when a key is pressed, a modulating LFO increases in level at a rate set by the user, causing the vibrato to build up naturally. It may also be possible to set a delay time so that the vibrato starts to build up a short time after the note is pressed, rather than straight away.

filtering

In addition to making emulations of acoustic instruments sound more realistic, filters are used extensively in the production of dance music to create resonant sweeps, dynamic bass sounds and percussive "thwips". If you're into dance music, you're going to need some VST instruments with good filter sections.

Taking natural emulations first, a plucked string produces a sound that's initially rich in high-frequency harmonics. Then, as the sound decays, the higher-frequency harmonics die away faster than the fundamental, producing a mellowing of tone as the volume decreases. A typical synth filter has one or more filter modes, the most important being Low Pass, and its cut-off frequency can be varied from a number of modulation sources – including envelopes and LFOs – to make this kind of effect possible. The cut-off frequency of a filter may also be controlled from a keyboard so that higher notes on the keyboard increase the filter frequency and vice versa.

More abstract filter settings use resonance to create the familiar wah-wah effect as the filter frequency is changed. Although a few real instruments share this characteristic, such as the muted trumpet, aggressive filter settings are normally used for the production of sounds that are deliberately synthetic.

Less sophisticated synths sometimes use the same envelope generator for controlling both the filter and the output level, while more comprehensive models have separate envelope generators for each section.

filter types

The majority of synthesiser filters are based around straightforward high-pass, bandpass or low-pass configurations, with low-pass being the most useful. However, it's possible to create more complex filter configurations, and some instruments are capable of using formant filtering to produce human vowel sounds and other effects.

A low-pass filter passes only frequencies below the frequency at which the filter is set and attenuates all higher frequencies. In other words, it cuts out the high frequencies and leaves the low frequencies intact. The slope or sharpness of the filter is usually 6dB, 12dB, 18dB or 24dB per octave, depending on the preferences of the designer. On an analogue instrument, the slope of the filter is fixed, whereas in a software plug-in, it's relatively simple to provide the user with a choice of

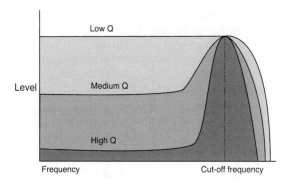

Figure 3.16: Low-pass filter with resonance

filter slopes, making it possible to emulate more closely the filter characteristics of analogue synthesisers from different manufacturers. The more decibels per octave, the sharper the effect of the filter.

So far, I've described the filter as a kind of EQ, but what makes it so creative is the addition of a Q or resonance control, which enables the filter to emphasise harmonics at the filter's cut-off frequency. When this frequency is changed, the resulting filter sweep sounds a little like a guitarist's wah-wah pedal at high Q settings. The graph in Figure 3.16 illustrates this effect. By adjusting the starting frequency of the filter, the frequency range over which it travels, the rate and direction of sweep and the resonance setting, it's possible to create a whole range of effects, from subtle to overtly synthetic.

filter modulation

The filter's frequency can be modulated from a number of sources, including (but not limited to) key note numbers, envelope generators and LFOs. It's also usually possible to invert the output of the envelope generator so that the filter sweeps from low to high instead of high to low, and on some instruments the amplitude and filter can be controlled by the same or separate envelope generators. Clearly, having separate envelope generators is a more flexible option. The combination of filter settings and the source waveform is the key to the timbre of analogue-style synthesisers, whereas with a sample-based model filter effects can be applied to any sound that the synthesiser can produce, from strings to bagpipes.

filter applications

There's more to using filters than creating dramatic filter sweeps. Sometimes you may only need to use a filter as a simple top-cut control to reduce the high-frequency content of a pad sound, or you may want to peak up the resonance slightly to emphasise some part of the audio spectrum without applying a sweep. In this case, no filter modulation is needed – you simply adjust the settings the way you want them. Meanwhile, adding MIDI Note control into the filter's control input makes the filter's frequency dependent on the note you're playing, which is useful if you're trying to simulate an instrument that sounds brighter on the higher notes than on the lower ones.

Brass-type sounds often use filter sweeps where the filter opens just quickly enough to add a fast "wah" to the attack of the sound, after which they close down again to give the sound a more mellow sustain. Brass patches are the easiest to produce, where separate envelope generators are used for both filter and level, although it's still possible to get reasonable brass sounds by using a single envelope generator. If the synth is analogue, you're probably only after the impression of a brass sound, whereas, if the synth is sample based, the chances are that you have a stock brass sound to work with anyway. In the latter case, you can use filtering to fine-tune the sound to suit your own needs.

The bass sounds on synths come in all shapes and sizes, but many are created in a similar way to the brass patch just described. The oscillators must be set to a lower octave, of course, and the choice of waveform will also make a large difference. Square and sawtooth waves produce harmonically rich sounds that respond well to filtering, while triangle waves are relatively pure and are best used to underpin a second oscillator or to create deep bass sounds with few harmonics. Sine waves may also be used to add depth, but remember that, when filtered, they'll change only in level, not sound.

The bass sounds used in dance music tend to make use of fast attack times, with the filter used to damp the sound as it closes. Faster attack and release times are useful when it comes to creating the tight, well-defined percussive bass sounds that work well on those songs where the bass line is used as a key rhythmic element.

In many analogue synth designs, the filter will go into self-oscillation at the maximum resonance setting, and in some instruments you can even use the oscillating filter as a separate tone source. Some digital instruments can also do this, but there's rarely a reason to do so, unless you're designing special effects. Most commonly used filter-sweep sounds use high Q settings, so that the filter is on the brink of oscillation, and the attack and release times are adjusted so that the rate of sweep suits the song. Very fast sweeps sound quite percussive and are good for use as techno "thwips", while longer sweeps are often used to enhance pad sounds.

Dance music often employs analogue-style sounds in which the filter settings (particularly the cut-off frequency) are adjusted manually in order to enhance the mood of the song. If you're using VST instruments, any changes to the synthesiser controls can be stored as MIDI data so that your moves can be played back later, complete with full automation. It's easy to automate one parameter at a time, by using the mouse to change control settings, but if you want to be able to change a number of parameters at once then you'll need a hardware MIDI controller fitted with sliders or knobs that produce MIDI controller data. Some of these come as presets for certain types of instrument, while others can be programmed to generate any MIDI controller message that's required. Alternatively, some controller keyboards come equipped with a number of assignable knobs or faders that can do the same thing. If dance music is your main area of interest, a hardware MIDI controller box or keyboard should be high on your list of priorities.

sample and hold

One interesting source of modulation often found in older analogue synthesisers is the S&H (sample-and-hold) generator. This works by sampling the output of the noise generator at intervals set by an LFO, and the result is a set of regularly spaced, random voltages that can be used to modulate things like oscillator pitch and filter frequency. Once again, this is an easy effect to replicate in a VST instrument plug-in, so if you have one with such a facility it's well worth playing around with it to find out what you can get out of it.

If the filter is adjusted to a fairly high Q setting and then modulated via the sample-and-hold generator, the result is a rhythmic "wah" effect that occurs as a series of steps. By synchronising the sample-and-hold generator to the song tempo (if you have that option), some very interesting rhythmic effects can be produced.

polyphony

In the analogue era, if you wanted more polyphony you'd have to duplicate almost all of a synth's circuitry for every voice, but in the world of VST instruments more polyphony just means using more

CPU power. All of the popular sequencers have some sort of CPU load meter, and this should always register under 80% in order to ensure reliable operation. By making sure that you're using no more polyphony than absolutely necessary is a good way of maximising your CPU resources. If you want to emulate an analogue monosynth, the polyphony value should be set to 1, which is also a useful setting for the production of dance bass lines and emulations of monophonic instruments.

on-board effects

The VST environment allows you to add extra plug-in effects to plug-in instruments, while a number of instruments include their own fully editable effects sections. Sometimes, these are very sophisticated – as in the case of Native Instruments' Reaktor and Dynamo plug-ins – and sometimes they can even be accessed as plug-in effects to treat other sound sources. However, the addition of effects invariably increases the demands on processor overhead, so don't be surprised to see your CPU meter showing an increase in load if you're using power-hungry effects such as reverb or some kind of complex modulation. The effects section of the Dynamo plug-in is shown in Figure 3.17.

basic VST instruments

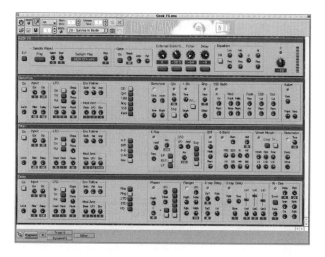

Figure 3.17: Effects section of Native Instruments' Dynamo plug-in

the user interface

The original analogue synthesisers had discrete knobs
and switches for every function so that, although they
looked daunting, at least you could go straight to any
parameter and adjust it. Hardware digital instruments
often look much simpler that this, but nevertheless all
of the parameters are still there, although they're often
hidden away in menus. Some of the current
instruments are designed with even more real knobs to

provide real-time control, but few provide direct access to everything.

VST instruments are operated via a virtual interface, which means that you can only adjust one parameter at a time with the mouse, but the chances are that the virtual control panel will show you all of the controls that you'll need to access, just on like those early analogue synths. For those situations where a single screen isn't enough to show all of the necessary parameters, there will be additional screens that you can flip between to make editing a relatively painless process.

Most VST instruments provide buttons for the selecting of patches and some have buttons to allow you to switch between the various banks of patches. Be aware, however, that these Bank Change buttons may be part of the VST instrument itself or, alternatively, they may be part of Cubase VST's Virtual Instrument window. If the latter is the case, users of other VST-compatible sequencers may not be able to access the additional banks. In my experience, this limitation arises mainly in VST instruments that have been marketed by Steinberg themselves.

Newly edited user patches can usually be named, and you may find that, in addition to the factory preset

Figure 3.18: TC Works' Mercury plug-in

sounds that load up when you first open the plug-in,
there are folders of additional sounds that can be
accessed by using the Open menu and then browsing to
the appropriate folders in the usual way. All user patches
are saved to your hard drive, and in most instances,
when you save a song, the VST instrument patch will be
saved along with it so that, when you re-open the song
at a later date, all of your VST instruments will be set up
correctly. However, there are some exceptions to this
rule, so you should read the manual that comes with
your VST instrument to see if this is the case.

modular instruments

There are a number of plug-ins currently available – including Reaktor – that will allow you to build your own synthesisers from separate modules that can then be patched together. A simpler approach is that adopted by TC Works with their Spark editing software, which includes a unique matrix into which VST effects and instruments can be placed. Their approach is to provide simple building blocks that the user can then patch together in the plug-in's FX Machine matrix to create a new instrument. Like traditional analogue synths, Spark Modular is monophonic, although, because it exists in a VST environment, other VST plug-ins can be inserted between the plug-in's modules to increase the sound-creation potential of the system. Complete instruments may then be saved and loaded into any Macintosh VST-compatible program as a single Spark FX Machine patch.

TC Works followed the success of their Modular system with a more ambitious analogue synthesiser emulation called Mercury, which is shown in Figure 3.18. Mercury uses a relatively high amount of CPU power, because it has very sophisticated modelled oscillators that, it's claimed, sound more "analogue" than sample-based waveforms.

basic VST instruments

Figure 3.19: Waldorf's Attack plug-in

synthetic drums

Electronic drum sounds are part of the modern musician's vocabulary, and many such sounds are based on discontinued electronic drum kits and beat boxes such as the Simmonds SDS5 and the Roland TR808 and TR909. Not surprisingly, there are VST plug-ins available that recreate the sounds of these old instruments, one of the most flexible being Waldorf Attack, shown in Figure 3.19. Each voice of the Attack plug-in has a similar

Figure 3.20: Steinberg's LM4 drum plug-in

structure, but it's flexible enough to recreate all of these classic sounds with a high degree of accuracy. It can also be used to create unique new percussion sounds, and it can even be used to produce conventional synth-style sounds such as pads and basses.

Steinberg's LM4 plug-in adopts a somewhat different approach by using sample-based drum sounds that the user can edit to only a very limited degree.

Figure 3.21: Emagic's EVP73 plug-in

Cosmetically, the plug-in looks like a drum machine, with 18 pads that can be used to trigger sounds, along with sliders for changing volume and tuning. The first bank of sounds is overtly electronic, while the remaining banks can be loaded with the high-quality drum samples that are included with the program. The LM4 is shown in Figure 3.20.

pianos

Pianos are traditionally recreated as sample-based voices, but Emagic's EVP73 uses physical-modelling techniques to emulate the sound and playing dynamics of a Fender Rhodes Suitcase electric piano. The EVP73 plug-in, shown here in Figure 3.21, models the physical responses of the metal tines being hit and dampened in these pianos, and the essential tremolo effect is also included as part of the plug-in. Because this instrument uses physical-modelling techniques, the dynamic response is much more natural than that of any sample-based electric piano.

samplers and sampling

A sampler is a type of synthesiser that enables the user to record and edit sound sources, although many users choose to use libraries of ready-made samples that are widely available on CD-ROM. On a hardware sampler, new pieces of audio are recorded into RAM and can then be played back at different pitches, under MIDI control. When a sample is replayed at a higher pitch than that at which it was recorded, the sampler speeds up the sound to bring it up to the right pitch, which also means that the sample plays back faster. Conversely, dropping the pitch necessitates slowing down the speed of the sample. This means that a little trickery has to be employed to keep the sound reasonably natural.

Note that RAM memory only stores information when powered up, so anything you've sampled that needs to be saved must be written to hard disk or some other storage device before you switch off your machine.

Figure 4.1: Sampletank's user interface

VST samplers work in essentially the same way as
their hardware counterparts, except that they use the
computer's own RAM to load and play back sounds
and the sound comes via the audio interface or
soundcard rather than from the back of an external
hardware unit. However, VST samplers have a
number of advantages over hardware models, not
least of which is that the user interface is often much
clearer. Also, as with other VST instruments, there's
no need to use complex multi set-ups for multitimbral
operation – you simply have to open a new sampler
on a new track each time you want to add a new part.
Figure 4.1 shows the user interface of Sampletank's
VST plug-in.

streaming

Conventional samplers hold all of their sounds in RAM, although a number of companies have now developed systems that allow sampled audio material to be streamed directly from a hard drive in much the same manner as a regular hard-disk recorder operates. Probably the best-known device in this area is the Tascam (formerly Nemesis) GigaSampler. On this machine, a short section at the start of each sample is held in RAM to enable the sampler to respond quickly when a note is played, after which the audio from the hard disk takes over. The obvious advantage with this technique is that you can use very large samples, which may be an advantage when using instruments such as grand pianos (as the sizes of samples are limited only by the available hard-drive space), but this is at the cost of increased hard-drive activity, which may reduce the number of conventional audio tracks that you can play back.

sampler applications

Hardware samplers tend to be used for two distinctly different types of job: to load instrument samples, whereupon they behave like a synthesiser but without the restricted repertoire; and to play back short loops of audio, such as a few bars of drums. Loop playback is managed so well by most sequencers that there's little need to use a sampler for this at all, although it's still perfectly possible, if you prefer to work in this way.

When using a sampler as a keyboard instrument, there is a limit on the amount of polyphony available, just as there is with synths, but in most cases you can specify the amount of polyphony you need. Beware, though, that increased polyphony eats up CPU power.

Owners of hardware samplers are always running out of memory, but a typical VST sampler uses a computer's own RAM for playback and, as I said, some are even able to stream audio samples directly from a hard drive, in which case the samples can be of almost any length. Computer memory is currently inexpensive, and the more you fit, the longer the samples you'll be able to play back. If you're using your sampler multitimbrally, the available sample memory is divided up between the various sounds you have loaded at any one time, so it soon gets used up. At a sampling rate of 44.1kHz, one minute of stereo sound takes up around 10MB of RAM.

looping

Earlier, I mentioned that some trickery was needed to gloss over the fact that samples play at different speeds at different pitches. Part of that strategy is to loop part of the sound, when the result is to be the sounds of sustaining parts such as strings, choirs or flutes. Sounds like pianos have a distinctive attack portion, but as they start to decay the sound becomes more consistent, making it possible to loop part of the decay in order to save on sample RAM. In effect, you simply sample the first few seconds of a note and then use the sampler's editing facilities to create a loop so that a section of the sample repeats itself continually until you release the key. Of course, when you buy samples on CD-ROM, all of this hard work is done for you.

Another good reason for looping sounds is to get around the length changes that occur when you play a sample higher or lower on the keyboard. If you didn't do this, the high notes would probably be very short. In any event, if you need a continuous pad or drone, you need to use a looped sample so that it plays indefinitely. Figure 4.2 shows how a sample loop is created.

crossfade looping

The trouble with looping is that, if you can't find a point in the sample where both ends of the loop match up perfectly, you'll probably end up with a click, at worst, or at best an abrupt change in tonality. Unless the waveform shapes at the beginning and end of the

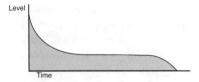

Shape of original sound

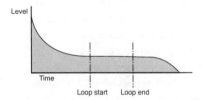

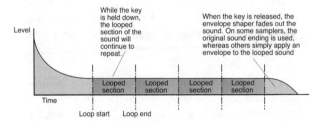

Behaviour of sound after looping

Figure 4.2: Looping a sustained sound

loop match up in level, shape and phase, you're quite likely to end up with a click. Clicks can be minimised by looping at zero-crossing points (ie the points at which the electrical signal crosses over from being positive to negative, or vice versa), but if the waveform levels and shapes don't match pretty closely, you may still hear a glitch.

Crossfade looping can help to disguise tricky loop points so that, instead of your loop point having a sudden transition between the beginning and the end, the start and end of the loop overlap slightly, with a smooth fade from one into the other. Ideally, the crossfade should be as short as possible while still being long enough to conceal the join. You also need to be careful when setting the loop length because, if the loop is too short, the sound will take on an irritating cyclic quality, especially at higher pitches, where the loop plays faster.

Conversely, if your loop is too long, you may find that the sound decays in level between the start and end of the loop to such a degree that the loop level is modulated in an unnatural way. Looping is an acquired skill, which is why most users leave it to professional sound designers and use sample-library CD-ROMs for their stock instrument sounds.

making your own samples

The way in which you record samples with a VST sampler will depend on the manufacturer of the plug-in. Some will allow you to sample directly using the VST sampler, whereas Emagic's EXS-24 VST, for example, requires you to record, trim and loop the samples in your host program's waveform editor before importing the result into the sampler. Once in the sampler, the loops can be crossfaded and the samples arranged into keygroups (ie groups of samples).

If you have an unusual instrument that you wish to sample, make the recording without adding vibrato or any other form of modulation, because not only would the modulation rate change depending on the playback pitch of the sample, but it's quite hard to loop a sample with vibrato. You'd have to find a good looping point that was also an exact multiple of the vibrato rate.

Stereo sounds are more difficult to loop than mono sounds, because you have to choose the same loop points for both channels. This can be tricky, as a good waveform match on one channel may not correspond to a good match on the other channel. Crossfade looping will probably be necessary to hide the loop point.

envelopes

Samplers include synth-style envelope shapers and also filters to allow you to modify your sampled sounds further. In most cases, the attack of the original sound can be left as it is, but the decay will often need to be adjusted so that the samples play naturally at any pitch. Instruments that sustain after the key is released can be handled in the Release phase of the envelope shaper, which uses the looped part of the sample as the sound decays.

triggering

Samplers tend to have a number of trigger modes so that they can handle not only routing instrument sounds but also drum and percussion sounds or rhythm loops. For example, if you hit the same key twice and you want the original sample to carry on to its natural conclusion while the newly triggered sound plays over the top, you need to select the "one-shot" trigger mode. On the other hand, if you want the original sound to stop and then trigger again from the beginning, as you might with a hi-hat or ride cymbal, you need to use the "retrigger" mode. Furthermore, if you're playing an open hi-hat followed by a closed hi-hat, you'll probably want the open hi-hat to cut off. Most samplers can deal with this, usually by assigning the hi-hat sounds to a group of their own, with the polyphony value set to 1. In this way, each new note played in that group will cut off the previous one.

multisampling

If you've tried to make any of your own samples, you'll certainly have noticed that most sounds become very unnatural when transposed too far away from their original pitches. This sometimes sounds interesting, in an abstract kind of way, but if you want a real instrument emulation to sound as accurate and convincing as possible then you'll need to use multisampling.

A sampled piano sounds natural for only a few semitones on either side of its original pitch, so the only way to get it sounding natural over the whole keyboard is to take several samples of the piano playing different notes at different points on the keyboard and then arrange these individual samples to play across the sampler's range, with no individual sample being moved more than a few semitones from its natural position.

This is the principle of multisampling, and the

sections of the keyboard covered by each sample are
known as *keygroups*. The more keygroups you have,
the more accurate the sound will be, but this means
that you'll need to record more samples, and this will
use up a lot of memory. Piano sounds are so critical, in
this respect, that I'd never recommend sampling one
yourself, unless you're doing it as an academic
exercise. Most other instruments can be shifted a little
further away from their original sounds before they
start to sound artificial, and you may be able to get
away with using just three or four individual samples.
Figure 4.3 shows the Keygroup window in Emagic's
EXS-24 plug-in.

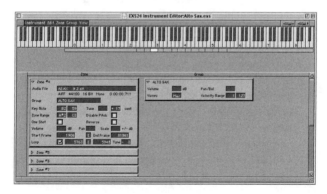

Figure 4.3: Keygrouping in Emagic's EXS-24 plug-in

velocity switching

Many instruments sound tonally different when they're played harder, so keyboard velocity isn't always the complete solution to natural dynamics. Instead, velocity switching or crossfading is used, which means having a separate loud and soft sample for each keygroup and then having the velocity of the key being pressed to determine which one plays at any one time. Velocity switching doesn't affect the overall polyphony, as only one sample plays at a time, but the transition between soft and loud may be too obvious. Crossfading to the louder sample sounds smoother, but it also halves the amount of polyphony available, as it means that two samples are playing at the same time.

samplers as phrase recorders

Since hardware samplers with lots of memory became available, it has become commonplace to sample whole musical phrases, which can then be played back on a single key. For example, you can play back one- or two-bar rhythm loops taken from other songs or from library disks or copy a good chorus from one part of a song and then trigger it whenever it's required. There's enormous creative potential in working in this way, but unless you need the pitch-shifting capabilities of a sampler then there's really little point in doing this within a sequencer environment, as the audio capabilities of the sequencer itself are more than capable of handling such routine work. However, a possible exception to this is when you have lots of phrases stored in the sampler and you want to experiment with the arrangement in real time.

looping drums

Some drum-loop sample sets are arranged in layers so that you can bring in different parts by hitting different keys, and it makes sense to use a sampler to perform this kind of application. However, you should always trigger the sample afresh every time it's needed rather than allow the sampler to create the loop, or you may find that, if the sampler tempo and loop tempo aren't perfectly matched, the timing drifts. In this case, simply retrigger your drum parts every bar or two, using a note from the sequencer quantised to the first beat of the bar. The same is true of other rhythmic elements such as guitar riffs, and even with long vocal sections it can be better to break them down into shorter phrases and then trigger each phrase independently.

sampling levels

Sampling audio into a computer is exactly the same as recording an audio track, so you should aim for the highest signal level possible without running into clipping in order to get the best results. Once the notes or phrases have been sampled, you can trim all of the starts and ends and normalise all of the levels, if necessary. If the samples are of single notes, you can also start to think about looping.

sample libraries

Not only are standard orchestral and instrumental sounds best obtained from a sound library, but you'll also find that so are a huge supply of grooves, loops, sound effects and samples of classic analogue synths. The most popular sample format at the moment is that of the Akai S1000 and S3000 machines, and most serious VST samplers can import these formats by using the computer's CD-ROM drive. There's also currently a trend towards supporting the less expensive SoundFont format developed by Creative Labs, as well as formats that are proprietary to other VST samplers. You'll probably be pleasantly surprised to find that sample sets that took an eternity to load into a hardware sampler via a CD-ROM drive will load into your VST sampler in seconds, once they've been transferred to your hard drive. If your VST sampler has the facility to create categories for your samples, I recommend that you make good use of it, or you'll soon find that your hard drive is cluttered with oddly named samples and you'll have no idea what they sound like.

Samples provided on CD-ROM are already set up in programs containing information concerning looping, key mapping, envelope settings and so on, so you really just need to load them and play. Meanwhile, samples in audio CD format are significantly cheaper than CD-ROM sample libraries. However, unless they're straightforward loops and breakbeats, you'll have to do all the trimming, looping and keygrouping yourself.

is VST the future?

VST is the closest thing we have to a standard for music software plug-ins, but it's by no means universally supported. A universal standard would be welcome, but there are so many conflicting commercial interests that this may never happen. Nevertheless, VST instruments and effects can be used with the majority of popular sequencer software packages on both Mac and PC (albeit sometimes with the aid of third-party "wrapper" software), and the sound quality is so good that manufacturers of hardware synths should be worrying more than they currently appear to be. Obviously, there are some hardware synths that don't yet have their software equivalents, but as more plug-ins appear on the market, and as computers continue to increase in power, the balance must eventually shift in favour of the software instrument. One thing is sure: the future is going to be a very exciting place!

common cable connections

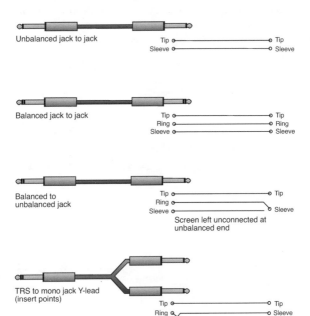

Unbalanced jack to jack

Tip ○————————○ Tip
Sleeve ○————————○ Sleeve

Balanced jack to jack

Tip ○————————○ Tip
Ring ○————————○ Ring
Sleeve ○————————○ Sleeve

Balanced to unbalanced jack

Tip ○————————○ Tip
Ring ○————————
Sleeve ○————————○ Sleeve

Screen left unconnected at unbalanced end

TRS to mono jack Y-lead (insert points)

Tip ○————————○ Tip
Ring ○————————○ Sleeve
Sleeve ○————————○ Tip
————————○ Sleeve

common cable connections

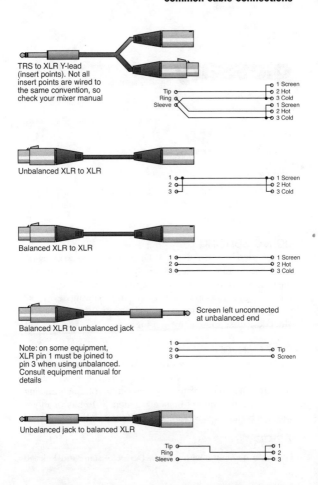

TRS to XLR Y-lead (insert points). Not all insert points are wired to the same convention, so check your mixer manual

Tip — 1 Screen / 2 Hot / 3 Cold
Ring — 1 Screen / 2 Hot / 3 Cold
Sleeve — 1 Screen / 2 Hot / 3 Cold

Unbalanced XLR to XLR

1 — 1 Screen
2 — 2 Hot
3 — 3 Cold

Balanced XLR to XLR

1 — 1 Screen
2 — 2 Hot
3 — 3 Cold

Balanced XLR to unbalanced jack

Screen left unconnected at unbalanced end

Note: on some equipment, XLR pin 1 must be joined to pin 3 when using unbalanced. Consult equipment manual for details

1 —
2 — Tip
3 — Screen

Unbalanced jack to balanced XLR

Tip — 1
Ring — 2
Sleeve — 3

glossary

AC
Abbreviation of Alternating Current.

active
Term used to describe a circuit that contains transistors, ICs, tubes and other devices that require power to operate and are capable of amplification.

active sensing
System used to verify that a MIDI connection is working, in which the sending device frequently sends short messages to the receiving device to reassure it that all is well. If these active sensing messages stop for any reason, the receiving device will recognise a fault condition and switch off all notes. Not all MIDI devices support active sensing.

A/D converter
Circuit for converting analogue waveforms into a series of values represented by binary numbers. The more bits a converter has the greater the resolution of the sampling process. Current effects units are generally 16 bits or more, with the better models being either 20 or 24 bit.

ADSR
Envelope generator with Attack, Decay, Sustain and Release

parameters. This is a simple type of envelope generator and was first used on early analogue synths, although similar envelopes may be found in some effects units to control filter sweeps and suchlike.

aftertouch

Means of generating a control signal based on how much pressure is applied to the keys of a MIDI keyboard. Most instruments that support this do not have independent pressure sensing for all keys but instead detect the overall pressure by means of a sensing strip running beneath the keys. Aftertouch may be used to control musical functions such as vibrato depth, filter brightness, loudness and so on, though it may also be used to control some parameter of a MIDI effects unit, such as delay feedback or effect level.

algorithm

Computer program designed to perform a specific task. In the context of effects units, the term usually describes a software building block designed to create a specific effect or combination of effects. All digital effects are based on algorithms.

aliasing

When an analogue signal is sampled for conversion into a digital data stream, the sampling frequency must be at least twice that of the highest frequency component of the input signal. If this rule is disobeyed, the sampling process becomes ambiguous, as there are insufficient points to define each waveform cycle, resulting in enharmonic sum and difference frequencies being added to the audible signal. (See "Nyquist Theorem".)

ambience

Result of sound reflections in a confined space being added to the original sound. Ambience may also be created electronically by some digital reverb units. The main difference between ambience and reverberation is that ambience doesn't have the characteristic long delay time of reverberation – the reflections mainly give the sound a sense of space.

amp
Standard unit of electrical current. The term *amp* is short for *ampère*.

amplitude
Another word for level. Can refer to levels of sound or electrical signal.

analogue
Term used to describe circuitry that uses a continually-changing voltage or current to represent a signal. The origin of the term lies in the fact that the electrical signal can be thought of as being analogous to the original signal.

anti-aliasing filter
Filter used to limit the frequency range of an analogue signal prior to A/D conversion so that the maximum frequency does not exceed half the sampling rate.

ASIO
Abbreviation of Audio Streaming Input/Output, an audio driver format introduced by Steinberg to accommodate low-latency routing between audio hardware and ASIO-compatible software.

attack
Time taken for a sound to achieve maximum amplitude.

Drums have a fast attack, whereas bowed strings have a slow attack. In compressors and gates, the attack time equates to how quickly the processor can change its gain.

attenuate
To make lower in level.

audio frequency
Signals in the human audio range, nominally between 20Hz and 20kHz.

aux
Control on a mixing console designed to route a proportion of the channel signal to the effects or cue mix outputs. (See "Aux Send".)

aux return
Mixer inputs used to add effects to the mix.

aux send
Physical output from a mixer aux send buss.

back-up
Safety copy of software or other digital data.

bandpass filter
Filter designed to remove or attenuate frequencies that lie above and below the frequency at which it is set while emphasising those that lie within the band. Bandpass filters are often found in synthesisers, where they're used as tone-shaping elements.

bandwidth

Means of specifying the range of frequencies passed by an electronic circuit such as an amplifier, mixer or filter. The frequency range is usually measured at the points where the level drops by 3dB relative to the maximum.

binary
Counting system based on a series of only two numbers: one and zero.

boost/cut control
Single control that allows the range of frequencies passing through a filter to be either amplified or attenuated. The centre position is usually the "flat" or "no effect" position.

bouncing
Process of mixing two or more recorded tracks together and re-recording these onto another track.

BPM
Abbreviation of Beats Per Minute.

breath controller
Device that converts breath pressure into MIDI controller data.

buffer
Circuit designed to isolate the output of a source device from loading effects due to the input impedance of the destination device.

buffer memory
Temporary RAM memory used in some computer operations, sometimes to prevent a break in the data stream when the computer is interrupted to perform another task.

buss

Common electrical signal path along which signals may travel. In a mixer, there are several busses carrying the stereo mix, the groups, the PFL signal, the aux sends and so on. Power supplies are also fed along busses.

channel

In the context of MIDI, the term *channel* refers to one of 16 possible data paths over which MIDI data may be sent. The organisation of data by channels means that up to 16 different MIDI instruments or parts may be addressed using a single cable.

channel

In the context of mixing consoles, a channel is a single strip of controls relating to one input.

chase

Term describing the process whereby a slave device attempts to synchronise itself with a master device. In the context of a MIDI sequence, Chase may also involve chasing events (looking back to earlier positions in the song to see if there are any program changes or other events that need to be acted upon).

chorus

Effect created by doubling a signal and adding delay and pitch modulation.

chromatic

Describes a scale of pitches rising in steps of one semitone.

clipping

Severe form of distortion that occurs when a signal attempts to exceed the maximum level that a piece of equipment can handle.

compander
Encode/decode device that compresses a signal while encoding it and then expands it when decoding it.

compressor
Device designed to reduce the dynamic range of audio signals by reducing the level of high signals or by increasing the level of low signals.

console
Alternative term for mixer.

continuous controller
Type of MIDI message used to translate continuous change, such as from a pedal, wheel or breath control device.

copy protection
Method used by software manufacturers to prevent unauthorised copying.

crash
Slang term used to describe a malfunction in a computer program.

cut-and-paste editing
Copying or moving sections of a recording to different locations.

cut-off frequency

Frequency above or below which attenuation begins in a filter circuit.

daisy chain

Term used to describe serial electrical connection between devices or modules.

damping

In the context of reverberation, damping refers to the rate at which reverberant energy is absorbed by the various surfaces in an environment.

DAT

Abbreviation of Digital Audio Tape. The most commonly-used DAT machines are more correctly known as R-DATs because they use a rotating head similar to that in a video recorder. Digital recorders using fixed or stationary heads (such as DCC) are known as S-DAT machines.

data

Information stored and used by a computer.

data compression

System for reducing the amount of data stored by a digital system. Most audio data-compression systems are known as lossy systems, because some of the original signal is discarded in accordance with psychoacoustic principles designed to ensure that only components that cannot be heard are lost.

dB

Abbreviation of Decibel. Unit used to express the relative levels of two electrical voltages, powers or sounds.

dB per octave

Means of measuring the slope of a filter. The more decibels per octave the sharper the filter slope.

DC

Abbreviation of Direct Current.

DCC

Stationary-head digital recorder format developed by Philips. Uses a data-compression system to reduce the amount of data that needs to be stored.

DDL

Abbreviation of Digital Delay Line.

decay

Progressive reduction in amplitude of a sound or electrical signal over time. In the context of an ADSR envelope shaper, the decay phase starts as soon as the attack phase has reached its maximum level. In the decay phase, the signal level drops until it reaches the sustain level set by the user. The signal then remains at this level until the key is released, at which point the release phase is entered.

de-esser

Device for reducing the effect of sibilance in vocal signals.

defragmentation

Process of rearranging the files on a hard disk so that all of the files are as contiguous as possible, and that the remaining free space is also contiguous.

digital

Term used to describe an electronic system that represents data and signals in the form of codes comprising ones and zeros.

digital delay
Digital processor for generating delay and echo effects.

digital reverb
Digital processor for simulating reverberation.

DIN connector
Consumer multipin signal connection format, also used for MIDI cabling. Various pin configurations are available.

direct coupling
Means of connecting two electrical circuits so that both AC and DC signals may be passed between them.

disc
Used to describe vinyl discs, CDs and MiniDiscs.

disk
Abbreviation of diskette now used to describe computer floppy, hard and removable disks. (See "Floppy Disk".)

dithering
System of adding low-level noise to a digitised audio signal in such a way as to extend low-level resolution at the expense of a slight increase in overall noise level.

DOS
Abbreviation of Disk Operating System, part of the operating system of PC and PC-compatible computers.

driver

Piece of software that handles communications between the main program and a hardware peripheral, such as a soundcard, printer or scanner.

drum pad

Synthetic playing surface that produces electronic trigger signals in response to being hit with drumsticks.

dry

Signal to which no effects have been added. Conversely, a sound that has been treated with an effect, such as reverberation, is referred to as wet.

DSP

Abbreviation of Digital Signal Processor, a powerful microchip used to process digital signals.

dubbing

Process of adding further material to an existing recording. Also known as overdubbing.

ducking

System for controlling the level of one audio signal with another. For example, background music can be made to duck whenever there is a voice-over.

dump

To transfer digital data from one device to another. A sysex (system-exclusive) dump is a means of transmitting information about a particular instrument or module over MIDI, and may be used to store sound patches, parameter settings and so on.

dynamic range
Range in decibels between the highest signal that can be handled by a piece of equipment and the level at which small signals disappear into the noise floor.

dynamics
Method of describing the relative levels within a piece of music.

early reflections
First sound reflections from walls, floors and ceilings following a sound that is created in an acoustically reflective environment.

effects loop
Connection system that allows an external signal processor to be connected into the audio chain.

effects return
Additional mixer input designed to accommodate the output from an effects unit.

effects unit
Device for treating an audio signal in order to change it in some creative way. Effects often involve the use of delay circuits, and include such treatments as reverb and echo.

enhancer
Device designed to brighten audio material using techniques such as dynamic equalisation, phase shifting and harmonic generation.

envelope

The way in which the level of a sound or signal changes over time.

envelope generator
Circuit capable of generating a control signal that represents the envelope of the sound to be recreated. This may then be used to control the level of an oscillator or other sound source, though envelopes may also be used to control filter or modulation settings. The most common example is the ADSR generator.

E-PROM
Similar to ROM, but in this case the information on the chip can be erased and replaced with the use of special equipment.

equaliser
Device for selectively cutting or boosting selected parts of the audio spectrum.

event
In MIDI terms, an event is a single unit of MIDI data, such as a note being turned on or off, controller information, a Program Change message and so on.

exciter
Enhancer that works by synthesising new high-frequency harmonics.

expander
Device designed to decrease the level of low-level signals and increase the level of high-level signals, thus increasing the dynamic range of the signal.

expander module

Synthesiser with no keyboard, often rack mountable or in some other compact format.

fader
Sliding potentiometer control used in mixers and other processors.

file
Meaningful list of data stored in digital form. A Standard MIDI File is a specific type of file designed to allow sequence information to be interchanged between different sequencers.

filter
Type of powerful tone-shaping network used in synthesisers to create tonal sweeps and wah-wah effects. The term filter may also be found in the manuals of some MIDI sequencers that are able to exclude or filter out certain types of MIDI data – for example, Aftertouch.

flanger
Short, pitch-modulated delay with feedback that, when added to the original signal, produces a deep comb-filtering effect reminiscent of tape phasing. Flanging is popular as a "psychedelic" effect.

floppy disk
Computer disk that uses a flexible magnetic medium encased in a protective plastic sleeve. The maximum capacity of a standard high-density disk is 1.44MB. Earlier double-density disks hold only around half that amount of data.

formant
Frequency component or resonance of an instrument or voice

sound that doesn't change with the pitch of the note being played or sung. For example, the body resonance of an acoustic guitar remains constant regardless of the note being played.

format

Procedure required to ready a computer disk for use. Formatting organises the disk's surface into a series of electronic pigeonholes into which data can be stored. Different computers often use different formatting systems.

fragmentation

Process by which the available space on a disk drive is split up into small sections due to the storing and erasing of files. (See "Defragmentation".)

frequency

Indication of how many cycles of a repetitive waveform occur in one second. A waveform that has a repetition cycle of once per second has a frequency of 1Hz.

frequency response

Measurement of the frequency range that can be handled by a specific piece of electrical equipment or loudspeaker.

fundamental

Any sound comprises a fundamental or basic frequency plus harmonics and partials at a higher frequency.

FX

Abbreviation of effects.

gain

Amount by which a circuit amplifies a signal.

gate

Electrical signal that is generated whenever a key is depressed on an electronic keyboard. This is used to trigger envelope generators and other events that need to be synchronised to key action.

gate

Electronic device designed to mute low-level signals, thus improving the noise performance during pauses in the wanted material.

General MIDI

Addition to the basic MIDI specification to assure a minimum level of compatibility when playing back GM-format song files. The specification covers type and program, number of sounds, minimum levels of polyphony and multitimbrality, response to controller information and so on.

glitch

Describes an unwanted short-term corruption of a signal, or the unexplained short-term malfunction of a piece of equipment. For example, an inexplicable click on a DAT tape would be termed a glitch.

graphic equaliser

Equaliser on which several narrow segments of the audio spectrum are controlled by individual cut/boost faders. The name derives from the fact that the fader positions provide a graphic representation of the EQ curve.

group

Collection of signals within a mixer that are mixed and then routed through a separate fader to provide overall control. In a multitrack mixer, several groups are provided to feed the various recorder track inputs.

GS
Roland's own extension to the General MIDI protocol.

hard disk
High-capacity computer storage device based on a rotating rigid disk with a magnetic coating onto which data may be recorded.

harmonic
High-frequency component of a complex waveform.

harmonic distortion
Addition of harmonics not present in the original signal.

head
Part of a tape machine or disk drive that reads and/or writes data to and from the storage media.

headroom
Safety margin in decibels between the highest peak signal being passed by a piece of equipment and the absolute maximum level the equipment can handle.

high-pass filter
Filter that attenuates frequencies below its cut-off frequency.

hiss
Noise caused by random electrical fluctuations.

hum

Signal contamination caused by the addition of low frequencies, usually related to the mains power frequency.

Hz
Abbreviation of Hertz, the unit of frequency.

insert point
Connector that allows an external processor to be patched into a signal path so that the signal then flows through the external processor.

interface
Device that acts as an intermediary to two or more other pieces of equipment. For example, a MIDI interface enables a computer to communicate with MIDI instruments and keyboards.

intermodulation distortion
Form of distortion that introduces frequencies not present in the original signal. These are invariably based on the sum and difference products of the original frequencies.

IRQ
Abbreviation of Interrupt Request, part of the operating system of a computer that allows a connected device to request attention from the processor in order to transfer data to it or from it.

jack
Common audio connector. May be mono (TS) or stereo (TRS).

k
Abbreviation of 1,000 (ie *kilo*). Used as a prefix to other values to indicate magnitude.

latency

Delay between the time audio enters a computer audio system and the time it becomes audible at the output. Latency is caused by the need to route audio via a computer's CPU, where buffers are used to ensure a constant stream of audio data. ASIO drivers minimise latency, but it can never be completely eradicated. If latency is below 7ms, it isn't considered to be a problem.

LCD

Abbreviation of Liquid Crystal Display.

LED

Abbreviation of Light-Emitting Diode, a solid-state lamp.

LFO

Abbreviation of Low-Frequency Oscillator, a device used as a modulation source, usually below 20Hz. The most common LFO waveshape is the sine wave, although many LFOs offer a choice of sine, square, triangular or sawtooth waveforms.

LSB

Abbreviation of Least Significant Byte. If a piece of data has to be conveyed as two bytes, one byte represents high-value numbers and the other low-value numbers, in much the same way as tens and units function in the decimal system. The high value, or most significant part of the message, is called the most significant byte, or MSB.

limiter

Device that controls the gain of a signal so as to prevent it from ever exceeding a preset level. A limiter is essentially a fast-acting compressor with an infinite compression ratio.

linear
Term used to describe a device on which the output is a direct multiple of the input.

line level
Mixers and signal processors tend to work at a standard signal level known as line level. In practice there are several different standard line levels, but all are in the order of a few volts. A nominal signal level is around -10dBv for semi-pro equipment and +4dBv for professional equipment.

load
Electrical circuit that draws power from another circuit or power supply. Also describes reading data into a computer.

load on/off
Function that allows the keyboard and sound-generating section of a keyboard synthesiser to be used independently of each other.

logic
Term used to describe a type of electronic circuitry used for processing binary signals comprising two discrete voltage levels.

loop
Circuit where the output is connected back to the input.

low-pass filter
Filter that attenuates those frequencies that occur above its cut-off frequency.

mA

Abbreviation of milliamp, or one thousandth of an amp.

MDM
Abbreviation of Modular Digital Multitrack, a digital recorder that can be used in multiples to provide a greater number of synchronised tracks than a single machine.

meg
Abbreviation of 1,000,000.

memory
Computer's RAM used to store programs and data. This data is lost when the computer is switched off and so must be stored to disk or other suitable media.

menu
List of choices presented by a computer program or a device with a display window.

mic level
Low-level signal generated by a microphone. This must be amplified many times to increase it to line level.

microprocessor
Specialised microchip at the heart of a computer. It is here that instructions are read and acted upon.

MIDI
Abbreviation of Musical Instrument Digital Interface.

MIDI analyser
Device that gives a visual readout of MIDI activity when connected between two pieces of MIDI equipment.

MIDI bank change

Type of controller message used to select alternate banks of MIDI programs where access to more than 128 programs is required.

MIDI controller

Term used to describe the physical interface by means of which the musician plays the MIDI synthesiser or other sound generator. Examples of controllers are keyboards, drum pads, wind synths and so on.

MIDI control change

Also known as MIDI controllers or controller data, these messages convey positional information relating to performance controls such as wheels, pedals, switches and other devices. This information can be used to control functions such as vibrato depth, brightness, portamento, effects levels, and many other parameters.

MIDI implementation chart

Chart usually found in MIDI product manuals that provides information as to which MIDI features are supported. Supported features are marked with a 0 while unsupported feature are marked with a X. Additional information may be provided, such as the exact form of the Bank Change message.

MIDI in

Socket used to receive information from a master controller or from the MIDI Thru socket of a slave unit.

MIDI merge

Device or sequencer function that enables two or more streams of MIDI data to be combined.

MIDI mode
MIDI information can be interpreted by the receiving MIDI instrument in a number of ways, and the most common of these is polyphonically, on a single MIDI channel (ie with the instrument in Poly/Omni Off mode). Omni mode enables a MIDI instrument to play all incoming data, regardless of channel.

MIDI module
Sound-generating device with no integral keyboard.

MIDI note number
Every key on a MIDI keyboard has its own note number, ranging from 0 to 127, where 60 represents middle C. Some systems use C3 as middle C while others use C4.

MIDI note off
MIDI message sent when key is released.

MIDI note on
Message sent when note is pressed.

MIDI out
MIDI connector used to send data from a master device to the MIDI In of a connected slave device.

MIDI port
MIDI connections of a MIDI-compatible device. A multiport, in the context of a MIDI interface, is a device with multiple MIDI output sockets, each capable of carrying data relating to a different set of 16 MIDI channels. Multiports are the only means of exceeding the limitations imposed by 16 MIDI channels.

MIDI program change
Type of MIDI message used to change sound patches on a remote module or the effects patch on a MIDI effects unit.

MIDI splitter
Alternative term for MIDI thru box.

MIDI sync
Description of the synchronisation systems available to MIDI users: MIDI clock and MIDI time code.

MIDI thru
Socket on a slave unit used to feed the MIDI In socket of the next unit in line.

MIDI thru box
Device that splits the MIDI Out signal of a master instrument or sequencer to avoid daisy chaining. Powered circuitry is used to "buffer" the outputs so as to prevent problems when many pieces of equipment are driven from a single MIDI output.

mixer
Device for combining two or more audio signals.

monitor
Reference loudspeaker used for mixing.

monitor
VDU for a computer.

monitoring
Action of listening to a mix or a specific audio signal.

monophonic

Term used to describe an instrument that plays only one note at a time.

motherboard

Main circuit board within a computer into which all the other components plug or connect.

MTC

Abbreviation of MIDI Time Code, a MIDI sync implementation based on SMPTE time code.

multisampling

Process of creating several samples, each covering a limited musical range, the idea being to produce a more natural range of sounds across the range of the instrument being sampled. For example, a piano may need to be sampled every two or three semitones in order to sound convincing.

multitimbral module

MIDI sound source capable of producing several different sounds at the same time and controlled on different MIDI channels.

multitrack

Recording device capable of recording several "parallel" parts or tracks which may then be mixed or re-recorded independently.

near field

Term used to describe a loudspeaker system designed to be positioned close to the listener and often called "close field". The advantage is that the listener hears more of the direct sound from the speakers and less of the reflected sound from the room.

noise reduction
System for reducing analogue tape noise or for reducing the level of hiss present in a recording.

noise shaping
System for creating digital dither so that any added noise is shifted into those parts of the audio spectrum where the human ear is least sensitive.

non-linear recording
Describes digital recording systems that allow any parts of the recording to be played back in any order with no gaps. Conventional tape is referred to as linear, because the material can only play back in the order in which it was recorded.

non-registered parameter number
Addition to the basic MIDI spec that allows controllers 98 and 99 to be used to control non-standard parameters relating to particular models of synthesiser. This is an alternative to using system-exclusive data to achieve the same ends, though NRPNs tend to be used mainly by Yamaha and Roland instruments.

normalise
A socket is said to be normalised when it is wired such that the original signal path is maintained, unless a plug is inserted into the socket. The most common examples of normalised connectors are the insert points on a mixing console.

Nyquist theorem
Rule that states that a digital sampling system must have a

sample rate at least twice as high as that of the highest frequency being sampled in order to avoid aliasing. Because anti-aliasing filters aren't perfect, the sampling frequency usually has to be made more than twice that of the maximum input frequency.

octave
When a frequency or pitch is transposed up by one octave, its frequency is doubled.

offline
Process carried out while a recording is not playing. For example, some computer-based processes have to be carried out offline as the computer isn't fast enough to carry out the process in real time.

ohm
Unit of electrical resistance.

open reel
Tape machine on which the tape is wound on spools rather than sealed in a cassette.

open circuit
Break in an electrical circuit that prevents current from flowing.

operating system
Basic software that enables a computer to load and run other programs.

opto-electronic device
Device on which some electrical parameters change in response to a variation in light intensity. Variable

photoresistors are sometimes used as gain control elements in compressors where the side-chain signal modulates the light intensity.

oscillator
Circuit designed to generate a periodic electrical waveform.

overdub
To add another part to a multitrack recording or to replace one of the existing parts. (See "Dubbing".)

overload
To exceed the operating capacity of an electronic or electrical circuit.

pad
Resistive circuit for reducing signal level.

pan pot
Control enabling the user of a mixer to move the signal to any point in the stereo soundstage by varying the relative levels fed to the left and right stereo outputs.

parallel
Method of connecting two or more circuits together so that their inputs and outputs are all connected together.

parameter
Variable value that affects some aspect of a device's performance.

parametric EQ
Equaliser with separate controls for frequency, bandwidth and cut/boost.

passive

Term used to describe a circuit with no active elements.

patch

Alternative term for program. The term *patch* refers to a single programmed sound within a synthesiser that can be called up using Program Change commands. MIDI effects units and samplers also have patches.

patch bay

System of panel-mounted connectors used to bring inputs and outputs to a central point from where they can be routed using plug-in patch cords.

patch cord

Short cable used with patch bays.

peak

Maximum instantaneous level of a signal.

peak

Highest signal level occurring in any section of programme material.

PFL

Abbreviation of Pre-Fade Listen, a system used within a mixing console that allows the operator to listen in on a selected signal, regardless of the position of the fader controlling that signal.

phantom power

48V DC supply for capacitor microphones, transmitted along the signal cores of a balanced mic cable.

phase
Timing difference between two electrical waveforms expressed in degrees, where 360° corresponds to a delay of one cycle.

phaser
Effect that combines a signal with a phase-shifted version of itself to produce creative filtering effects. Most phasers are controlled by means of an LFO.

phono plug
Hi-fi connector developed by RCA and used extensively on semi-pro, unbalanced recording equipment.

pick-up
Part of a guitar that converts string vibrations to electrical signals.

pitch
Musical interpretation of an audio frequency.

pitch bend
Special control message specifically designed to produce a change in pitch in response to the movement of a pitch bend wheel or lever. Pitch bend data can be recorded and edited, just like any other MIDI controller data, even though it isn't part of the controller message group.

pitch shifter
Device for changing the pitch of an audio signal without changing its duration.

plug-in
Software designed to add functionality to a host program – for example, a VST effect or instrument.

polyphony

Term used to describe an instrument's ability to play two or more notes simultaneously. An instrument that can play only one note at a time is described as monophonic.

port

Connection for the input or output of data.

portamento

Gliding effect that allows a sound to change pitch at a gradual rate rather than abruptly when a new key is pressed or MIDI note sent.

post-production

Work that's carried out on a stereo recording after mixing is complete.

post-fade

Aux signal taken from after the channel fader so that the aux send level follows any channel fader changes. Normally used for feeding effects devices.

power supply

Unit designed to convert mains electricity to the voltages necessary to power an electronic circuit or device.

PPM

Peak Programme Meter, a meter designed to register signal peaks rather than the average level.

PPQN

Abbreviation of Pulses Per Quarter Note. Used in the context of MIDI-clock-derived sync signals.

PQ coding
Process for adding pause, cue and other subcode information to a digital master tape in preparation for CD manufacture.

pre-emphasis
System for applying high-frequency boost to a sound before processing so as to reduce the effect of noise. A corresponding de-emphasis process is required on playback so as to restore the original signal and to attenuate any high-frequency noise contributed by the recording process.

pre-fade
Aux signal taken from before the channel fader so that the channel fader has no effect on the aux send level. Normally used for creating foldback or cue mixes.

preset
Effects unit or synth patch that cannot be altered by the user.

pressure
Alternative term for aftertouch.

processor
Device designed to treat an audio signal by changing its dynamics or frequency content. Examples of processors include compressors, gates and equalisers.

program change
MIDI message that changes instrument or effects unit patches.

pulse wave
Similar to a square wave but non-symmetrical. Pulse waves sound brighter and thinner than square waves, making them

useful in the synthesis of reed instruments. The timbre of the sound changes according to the mark/space ratio of the waveform.

pulse-width modulation
Means of modulating the duty cycle (mark/space ratio) of a pulse wave. This changes the timbre of the basic tone. LFO modulation of pulse width can be used to produce a pseudo-chorus effect.

punch-in
Action of placing an already recorded track into record at the correct time during playback so that the existing material may be extended or replaced.

punch-out
Action of switching a tape machine (or other recording device) out of record after executing a punch in. With most multitrack machines, both punching in and punching out can be accomplished without stopping the tape.

Q
Measurement of the resonant properties of a filter. The higher the Q, the more resonant the filter and the narrower the range of frequencies that are allowed to pass.

quantising
Means of moving notes recorded in a MIDI sequencer so that they line up within user-defined subdivisions of a musical bar – for example, 16th notes (semiquavers). The facility may be used to correct timing errors, but over-quantisation can remove the human feel from a performance.

RAM
Abbreviation of Random Access Memory. This is a type of memory used by computers for the temporary storage of programs and data, and all data is lost when the power is turned off. For that reason, work needs to be saved to disk if it is not to be lost.

R-DAT
Digital tape machine using a rotating head system.

real time
Audio process that can be carried out as the signal is being recorded or played back. The opposite is off-line, where the signal is processed in non-real time.

release
Time it takes for a level or gain to return to normal. Often used to describe the rate at which a synthesised sound reduces in level after a key has been released.

resistance
Opposition to the flow of electrical current. Measured in ohms.

resolution
Accuracy with which an analogue signal is represented by a digitising system. The more bits are used, the more accurately the amplitude of each sample can be measured, but there are other elements of converter design that also affect accuracy. High conversion accuracy is known as high resolution.

resonance
Characteristic of a filter that allows it to selectively pass a narrow range of frequencies. (See "Q".)

reverb
Acoustic ambience created by multiple reflections in a confined space.

RF
Abbreviation of Radio Frequency.

RF interference
Interference that takes place significantly above the range of human hearing.

ribbon microphone
Microphone in which the sound-capturing element is a thin metal ribbon suspended in a magnetic filed. When sound causes the ribbon to vibrate, a small electrical current is generated within the ribbon.

ring modulator
Device that accepts and processes two input signals in a particular way. The output signal doesn't contain any of the original input signals but instead comprises new frequencies based on the sum and difference of the input signals' frequency components. The results may be either musical or extremely dissonant, depending on the relationships between the input signals – for example, ring modulation can be used to create bell-like tones. (The term ring is used in this instance because the original circuit that produced the effect used a ring of diodes.)

RMS
Abbreviation of Root Mean Square, a method of specifying the behaviour of a piece of electrical equipment under continuous sine wave testing conditions.

roll-off
Rate at which a filter attenuates a signal once it has passed the filter cut-off point.

ROM
Abbreviation of Read-Only Memory. This is a permanent and non-volatile type of memory containing data that cannot be changed. Operating system software is often stored on ROM as the memory remains intact when the power is switched off.

sampling
Process carried out by an A/D converter where the instantaneous amplitude of a signal is measured many times per second (44.1kHz in the case of CD).

sample
Digitised sound used as a musical sound source in a sampler or additive synthesiser.

sample and hold
Usually refers to a feature whereby random values are generated at regular intervals and then used to control another function such as pitch or filter frequency. Sample and hold circuits were also used in old analogue synthesisers to "remember" the note being played after a key had been released.

sample rate
Number of times that an A/D converter samples the incoming waveform each second.

sawtooth wave
So called because it resembles the teeth of a saw, this waveform contains only even harmonics.

SCSI
Abbreviation of Small Computer System Interface, pronounced "skuzzi". An interfacing system for using hard drives, scanners, CD-ROM drives and similar peripherals with a computer. Each SCSI device has its own ID number and no two SCSI devices in the same chain must be set to the same number. The last SCSI device in the chain should be terminated either via an internal terminator, where provided, or via a plug-in terminator fitted to a free SCSI socket.

sequencer
Device for recording and replaying MIDI data, usually in a multitrack format, allowing complex compositions to be built up a part at a time.

short circuit
Low-resistance path that allows electrical current to flow. The term is usually used to describe a current path that exists through a faulty condition.

sibilance
High-frequency whistling or lisping sound that affects vocal recordings due either to poor mic technique or excessive equalisation.

side chain
Part of a circuit that splits off a proportion of the main signal to be processed in some way. Compressors use a side-chain signal to derive their control signals.

signal
Electrical representation of input such as sound.

signal chain

Route taken by a signal from the input of a system to its output.

signal-to-noise ratio

Ratio of maximum signal level to the residual noise, expressed in decibels.

sine wave

Waveform of a pure tone with no harmonics.

single-ended noise reduction

Device for removing or attenuating the noise component of a signal. Doesn't require previous coding, as in the case of Dolby or dbx.

slave

MIDI device under the control of a master device, such as a sequencer or master keyboard.

SMPTE

Time code developed for the film industry but now extensively used in music and recording. SMPTE is a real-time code and is related to hours, minutes, seconds and film or video frames rather than to musical tempo. SMPTE stands for the Society of Motion Picture and Television Engineers.

SPL

Sound-Pressure Level. Measured in decibels.

SPP

Song-Position Pointer (MIDI).

square wave

Symmetrical rectangular waveform. Square waves contain a series of odd harmonics.

step time
System for programming a sequencer in non-real time.

stereo
Two-channel system feeding left and right loudspeakers.

stripe
To record time code onto one track of a multitrack tape machine.

sub-bass
Frequencies below the range of typical monitor loudspeakers. Some define sub-bass as frequencies that can be felt rather than heard.

subcode
Hidden data within the CD and DAT format that includes such information as the absolute time location, number of tracks, total running time and so on.

subtractive synthesis
Process of creating a new sound by filtering and shaping a raw, harmonically complex waveform.

surge
Sudden increase in mains voltage.

sustain
Part of the ADSR envelope that determines the level to which the sound will settle if a key is held down. Once the key is

released, the sound decays at a rate set by the release parameter. Also refers to a guitar's ability to hold notes that decay very slowly.

sweet spot
Optimum position for a microphone or a listener relative to monitor loudspeakers.

switching power supply
Type of power supply that uses a high-frequency oscillator prior to the transformer so that a smaller, lighter transformer may be used. These power supplies are commonly used in computers and some synthesiser modules.

sync
System for making two or more pieces of equipment run in synchronism with each other.

synthesiser
Electronic musical instrument designed to create a wide range of sounds, both imitative and abstract.

tape head
Part of a tape machine that transfers magnetic energy to the tape during recording or reads it during playback.

tempo
Rate of the beat of a piece of music, measured here in beats per minute.

test tone
Steady, fixed-level tone recorded onto a multitrack or stereo recording to act as a reference when matching levels.

timbre
Tonal "colour" of a sound.

track
Term that dates back to multitrack tape, on which the tracks are physical stripes of recorded material located side by side along the length of the tape.

tracking
System whereby one device follows another. Tracking is often discussed in the context of MIDI guitar synthesisers or controllers where the MIDI output attempts to track the pitch of the guitar strings.

transducer
Device for converting one form of energy into another. A microphone is a good example of a transducer, as it converts mechanical energy to electrical energy.

transparency
Subjective term used to describe audio quality where the high-frequency detail is clear and individual sounds are easy to identify and separate.

transpose
To shift a musical signal by a fixed number of semitones.

tremolo
Modulation of the amplitude of a sound using an LFO.

triangle wave
Symmetrical, triangle-shaped wave that contains only odd harmonics and has a lower harmonic content than a square wave.

TRS jack
Stereo-type jack with tip, ring and sleeve connections.

unison
To play the same melody using two or more different instruments or voices.

valve
Vacuum-tube amplification component, also known as a tube.

velocity
Rate at which a key is depressed. This may be used to control loudness (to simulate the response of instruments such as pianos) or other parameters on later synthesisers.

vibrato
Pitch modulation using an LFO to modulate a VCO.

vocoder
Signal processor that imposes a changing spectral filter on a sound based on the frequency characteristics of a second sound. By taking the spectral content of a human voice and imposing it on a musical instrument, talking instrument effects can be created.

voice
Capacity of a synthesiser to play a single musical note. An instrument capable of playing 16 simultaneous notes is said to be a 16-voice instrument.

volt
Unit of electrical power.

VST

Abbreviation of Virtual Studio Technology, a Steinberg protocol that allows a common range of plug-in effects and instruments to be used with VST-compatible host software.

VU meter

Meter designed to interpret signal levels in roughly the same way as the human ear, which responds more closely to the average levels of sounds rather than to the peak levels.

wah-wah pedal

Guitar effects device in which a bandpass filter is varied in frequency by means of a pedal control.

warmth

Subjective term used to describe sound in which the bass and low-mid frequencies have depth and the high frequencies are smooth sounding, rather than aggressive or fatiguing. Warm-sounding tube equipment may also exhibit some of the aspects of compression.

watt

Unit of electrical power.

waveform

Graphic representation of the way in which a sound wave or electrical wave varies with time.

watt

Unit of electrical power.

white noise

Random signal with an energy distribution that produces the same amount of noise power per Hz.

XG
Yamaha's alternative to Roland's GS system for enhancing the General MIDI protocol so as to provide additional banks of patches and further editing facilities.

XLR
Type of connector commonly used to carry balanced audio signals, including the feeds from microphones.

Y-lead
Lead split so that one source can feed two destinations. Y-leads may also be used in console insert points, when a stereo jack plug at one end of the lead is split into two monos at the other.

zero crossing point
Point at which a signal waveform crosses from being positive to negative and vice versa.

zipper noise
Audible steps that occur when a parameter is being varied in a digital audio processor.